Happy
Birthday
Dr. Miller,
May your day be filled
with blessings. ♡
Jan

I pray this little
book I wrote blesses
you as much as the
hospice journey blessed
me.
With Love
JK Johnson

JOURNEY
TO
THE *Edge*
of Heaven

J K JOHNSON

WESTBOW
PRESS®
A DIVISION OF THOMAS NELSON
& ZONDERVAN

This book is a work of non-fiction. Unless otherwise noted, the author and the publisher make no explicit guarantees as to the accuracy of the information contained in this book and in some cases, names of people and places have been altered to protect their privacy.

WestBow Press books may be ordered through booksellers or by contacting:

WestBow Press
A Division of Thomas Nelson & Zondervan
1663 Liberty Drive
Bloomington, IN 47403
www.westbowpress.com
1 (866) 928-1240

ISBN: 978-1-5127-9462-5 (sc)
ISBN: 978-1-5127-9463-2 (hc)
ISBN: 978-1-5127-9461-8 (e)

Library of Congress Control Number: 2017910996

Print information available on the last page.

WestBow Press rev. date: 7/18/2017

I dedicate this book to my three wonderful boys, Andy, Matti, and Christopher, who unselfishly shared their mom with her hospice patients for eleven years, who, without complaining, would get out of their warm bed to go sleep in the van, when I would be paged out in the middle of the night. Thank you, boys, for your soft hearts and understanding. You will never know what it meant to me and how much I love you. Remember to always follow your heart and listen to the Lord.

PS: Boys, want to go to dinner? I'm on call. You had better grab your sleeping bags.

In memory of Allison Renae and Honey, who left paw prints in my heart forever and in the hearts of the patients we shared. You are loved and missed.

A special dedication to Shannon and Pearl, two very beautiful women both inside and out. I love you with all my heart. Where would I be without you two? May God hold you both in the palms of his hands.

A special thank-you to all my patients and their families for the lessons learned and memories we shared. You will always hold a special place in my heart until we meet again.

CONTENTS

Introduction ix

1. Susan's Smile 1

2. On Hallowed Ground 8

3. Jesus as an Old Guy 19

4. Is Anyone Going to Answer the Phone? 29

5. Have You Read the Newspaper This Morning? 37

6. The Curmudgeon 44

7. You're Not Going to Believe Who I Just Talked To 60

8. For Every Life You Have Ever Touched 73

9. Through the Eyes of a Child 88

A Note From the Author 99

About the Author 101

INTRODUCTION

For years friends and family encouraged me to write a book about the experience of death through a hospice nurse's eyes. It wasn't until God started insisting over and over that I share my experiences with all of you that the decision was made that I had better listen. God wanted me to share with you the amazing change He made in my life. As a young adult, I feared death and didn't understand heaven. I could not get the answers I needed from those who should have had them. I just knew there was more. I prayed to God often about my fears and want for answers. I believe this is how He answered me.

I was working at a nursing facility the local hospice nurses frequented often to see their patients. One day, when the hospice boss herself came to see one of the patients, she offered me a job, stating, "We would like you on our team. Are you interested in working for hospice?"

I quickly responded with a smile, "Oh no, you don't know me. I don't do well with death. I avoid it if I can."

So a few months later, when the boss herself came back to see one of the hospice patients, she again asked me if I would like to work for them. She was offering me a job. She thought I was exactly what they were looking for. Very quickly, I thanked her for the compliment and said how sorry I was, but this nurse could never, ever work with death every day, and they had the wrong girl. Now is when I believe the Lord had to give this situation more of a push, because He knew my conscience. A few things happened at work, and being a good Christian, it made it impossible for me to continue to work for that company any longer. What was I going to do? I had never been without a job. I just did as always—prayed and left it in God's hands.

Before long the hospice boss was in seeing one of her patients, and before she left, she stopped and said, "I am going to ask you to come work with us one more time. Then I won't bother you anymore."

To her surprise, I said yes, but I followed up with, "Remember, I don't do death, and I will continue to look for another job, so don't put much time or effort into me please."

She just smiled and said, "We will see. I think you are our girl, and I think you will be just fine."

So when it was final and the job was mine, the Lord

took over, and what He revealed to me in those eleven years is simply amazing. The Lord answered my prayers. I am no longer scared of death. It is my comfort zone.

So now my prayer for all of you is that when you finish reading my book, you will have a little more peace in your heart about what that final journey on this earth looks like from just this side of the edge of heaven. I am not saying it will make it any easier to lose your loved one, but it may ease your mind when I tell you what God has revealed to me in my eleven years as a hospice nurse.

1

Susan's Smile

I would like you to meet Susan. She was one of my first cancer patients I had the pleasure of taking care of. We had become very good friends over the past few months. During that time, Susan could tell that my heart was quietly aching at the thought of losing her. In her own sweet way, she was trying to teach me that death was not such a bad thing and that there were worse things in life than dying. Susan for one was not afraid to die, and she would tell you she was ready any time her Lord called her home. Susan was, however, tired of being alone. Susan had no family left in the physical world: her parents were gone, her husband had died suddenly of a heart attack a few years back, and their only daughter was killed in an auto accident at a very young age. Susan had nothing left to keep her alive.

Before long, Susan began to decline rapidly; the

cancer had begun to take over. Her prayers to go home were about to become a reality. I happened to be the hospice nurse on call, and I was nervous. What was God thinking? I was too close to Susan to be the nurse for the end stages of her life. I was about to lose my first patient and my special friend. My heart was aching. *I don't think I can do this*, I thought. I was there all alone, and what Susan needed was a well-seasoned, calm nurse. I prayed for God to stay close, as I was sure he always did, but with my nerves I was having trouble feeling his presence right then. I was all Susan had, and she deserved the best, so I prayed that God would wrap his mighty arms around us as I walked with her on her journey that day.

Looking back, I believe God had that day planned; He knew exactly what I was about to see and experience. He orchestrated every single moment of that day. He laid the groundwork for what I was going to see and experience for the next eleven years as a hospice nurse. Let me share with you Susan's amazing final journey.

I had the privilege of sitting quietly beside my patient's bed, holding her frail, cool hand as she drifted in and out of sleep. The room was dim, the afternoon sun had set, and night was fast approaching. A sweet fragrance filled the air, emanating from a beautiful bouquet of flowers that adorned the bedside table. The flowers had been hand-delivered by a lifelong friend of the patient's, who had come for what would be her last visit earlier that day.

Susan was getting very close to the end of her long journey. The telltale signs were all there: her vital signs were changing, and her breathing was becoming slower, more irregular, and occasionally absent. When I had done my last assessment, I noted some discoloration on her feet and legs. She was cool to the touch from her feet to her knees. I was new at being a hospice nurse and assessing the dying patient, but I had seen enough to know that her time was getting short. I began to pray for God to stay close by—and to help me. I was scared, and I needed Him to walk with me as I took each step of this journey with my precious Susan.

As I continued to sit quietly by her bed, she was drifting in and out of sleep. When she would wake, she would look around with amazement and with eyes wide open, and then she would begin to explain to me what she was seeing: beautiful visions of a place that seemed unreal, with colors so vivid they almost took her breath away. Each time she would wake, she would explain what she saw. The view from where she was at that moment was too beautiful for words. I thought, *Wow, is she seeing heaven?* Then I remembered 2 Corinthians 3:16: "But whenever anyone turns to the Lord, the veil is taken away." Because she was so close to dying and looking toward her Lord, the veil had been made thin and she could see into heaven. Amazing!

Then out of nowhere, she stopped talking, looked

up to the right corner of the room, and eagerly greeted someone whom I could not see. "Oh, Trish, I can't believe it's you! I have missed you; I will be with you soon."

I sat quietly and listened to the one-sided, excited, tearful conversation that seemed to go on forever. When she was finished, she looked at me, the tearful smile faded, and she said, "You aren't going to believe who I just talked to, but I have to tell someone."

I said, "Of course; you can tell me anything."

She hesitantly uttered the words, "That was my daughter. I lost her several years ago in an auto accident. I can't believe she was here. She is waiting for me to come home. You do believe me, don't you?"

I swallowed hard, smiled, and said, "Well, of course I believe you."

Shortly, the patient fell back to sleep, and again I began to pray. The half of the conversation I had heard had been so real that I knew she was talking to someone. Could she have been talking to angels? Then I thought, *She is seeing so many beautiful visions. Is the veil that thin? Is she really that close to the end of her journey? Could she really see into heaven? Lord, I have so many questions.*

Soon she woke from a long nap, and with a weak voice she shared the beautiful visions she was enjoying. Each vision was a little different and more spectacular than the last; she exclaimed how her visions were in colors never envisioned down here. Once again, her attention was drawn to the right-hand corner of the room. She was very weak but very excited to see this person.

"Hello, John. Are you here to take me home? I saw our Trish a little while ago; she is whole again, John. Take me home with you—I'm ready."

This time I was calmer and accepting, and I could listen with a little of her excitement. When she had finished, she couldn't wait to tell me that the visitor she talked to was her husband. The visions slowed, and the visitors came and went very quickly for a while. It didn't take me long to become comfortable with all the "angels" appearing in her room.

During all my visits with her over the previous months, she had talked about being ready to die. It was hard for me to hear that—and she knew it. She would always tell me, "I am tired of being sick, I have no family left down here, and I am ready to go home to be with my Lord. Please don't wish me to stay here any longer than I have to."

I always said I wouldn't, but we had become so close that I couldn't bear the thought of her death. My heart was aching at the thought of losing her. What was God thinking, placing me here at her death! However, without even realizing it—and because of her visions and visitors throughout the day—I was starting to get excited for her to go home and be with the Lord.

Meanwhile, Susan was becoming so weak; clearly

the end was very near. She wasn't talking as much. She would look around and smile, or point, and I would know what she meant. I reached over and held her frail hand as she fell fast asleep. As I watched her sleep, I prayed and thanked God for making sure this was where I was that day and trusting me enough to show me that she was going to a better place. I realized that my wanting her to stay here was selfish. As the Bible says, the veil is very thin at the end, and that had been proven to me over and over that day to be true.

Finally, my precious little angel woke from one of her short rests. Her eyes widened, she looked over at me for what would be the last time, and she looked back at the corner of the room. The most glorious smile came over her face, and she said with a full voice, "There He is." Her eyes shut, her hand went limp in mine, and she was gone. I looked at the place where her eyes had been directed, but I could see nothing. Tears ran down my cheeks as I stood there in the quiet, dimly lit room, and then I realized I was standing on hallowed ground, because the Lord had just been in the room. I wanted so badly for her to open her eyes one more time and tell me what He looked like, but she was gone. She was now healed and at the right hand of the Lord in heaven. I kissed her on the cheek and whispered good-bye. Then for the first time, I thanked God for this job. I finally understood what my purpose was. I had just walked my first patient to the edge of heaven and handed her off to the Lord. I did not know it at the time, but God had only just begun to show me what He wanted me to learn from this journey.

The next day, the local mortuary that had picked up Susan called just to let me know that the smile the patient seemed to have on her face when they picked her up at her home was still on her face when they got her to the funeral home. They knew I was close to the patient, and they thought telling me that would bring a smile to my day. I thanked them and told them it did make me smile, but what I didn't tell them was that her beautiful smile was there because her last vision was of the Lord's face. I figured it could be our secret—right, Susan!

But whenever anyone turns to the Lord, the veil is taken away. (2 Corinthians 3:16, New Women's Devotional Bible)

2

On Hallowed Ground

It was late fall, and the holidays were upon us. A slight chill filled the air, and the aroma of burning wood from a fireplace was almost intoxicating. It wrapped around you like a warm blanket. I loved it here and had come to the conclusion that I would be a forever tourist. The weather was so beautiful this time of year. Where I grew up, we would have been in winter coat and mittens by now. Burr, the mere thought of it could still make me shiver even after all these years.

I had finally arrived at the assisted living complex where my patient, Mary, lived. The assisted living complex was nestled deep among the majestic pines. This home, with its diverse individuals, offered something for everyone. If you felt like an adventure, you could take the path of plush green grass leading down to a slow, meandering river and go fishing. You could take a short hike in the woods or just sit on a bench or porch swing and watch the wildlife wander by. You could also do like most of them did and just sit out on the patio watching the clouds float slowly by over the mountaintop. Wherever you looked outside, you could see God's handiwork, and giving thanks came easy. This place was amazing.

As I entered the building, the delicious smell of lunch made me hungry. I didn't realize it was already that time of day. I said hi to some of the friendly caregivers on my way to Mary's room. The caregivers in this facility were outstanding. They really had good hearts, and the residents were well taken care of. I always felt that the caregivers treated them like family, which was good, because unfortunately all too often, all some of them had for family was their caregiver and the facility's staff.

As I got to Mary's room, she was sound asleep on her bed. I sat down quietly on a chair beside her bed and looked around at all the wonderful memories she and her daughter had arranged so beautifully around the room and that hung in frames on the wall. Mary had been married to her beloved husband for sixty years, and together, they had two loving children. Mary's husband had died two years ago, and her broken heart had just never healed. When Mary was diagnosed with cancer, it wasn't long before it become unsafe for her to stay alone anymore. So, Mary, like so many, had to downsize her entire life to just what would fit into this small little one bedroom studio. Mary agreed her new place was beautiful, but would say, "It's just not home". Mary often said nothing would ever feel like home until she was with her husband again, and that would be when she went home to be with Jesus in Heaven.

As I sat there quietly beside her bed, I began to chart how Mary looked this visit, how her color was, her breathing, had she lost more weight ... Then suddenly, Mary excitedly proclaimed, "My Mother is here. She said she likes you, and thinks you are very sweet." I nearly jumped out of my skin! Mary had startled me. I said quietly, "Oh, I'm sorry did I wake you?" Mary had rolled over, and was facing me. She looked up at me, and asked, "Do you believe my Mother is here"? I had been in this job several months by now, but to be honest those words still took me by surprise. But I was not about to let Mary think I did not believe her. I was very aware of angels visiting the dying, so I smiled and said, "Yes, of course I believe you, Mary, and I am very happy she likes me." I leaned over her bed and gave her a kiss on her forehead.

Mary gave me one of her precious smiles that melted my heart, and her eyes filled with tears as she said, "If I could only share those moments with my daughter before I die."

I sat down beside her bed and took Mary's hand. I was wondering what she had meant by that statement. Mary began to explain how her children had stopped coming to see her. They told their mother how they could not stand to see her sick anymore, so they were going to stop their visits. They told her it would be more than they could handle to watch her die, so they wanted to remember her like she was. They would not be back to see her anymore. They would call her on the phone while she could still manage, but they did not want to talk about her illness. Mary was lying on her bed looking up at the ceiling while she was talking to me, which was a good thing because the tears were just streaming down my face. I could not wrap my head around what she was telling me. What was wrong with these grown children hurting their precious mother like this? They knew how far along their mother was in her disease process. Why were they doing this?

Mary's cancer was advancing more rapidly in the last month, and our visits had been increased to at least three times per week. I thought it was strange that none of the hospice nurses had run into any of her family during our visits. Well, this was why. They had stopped coming to visit their mother.

Mary tightened her grip on my hand and continued to talk. "When I was first diagnosed with cancer, I was devastated. Then I found out there wasn't anything they could do for it, and I completely shut down for a little while. Then I began to pray and found peace. My kids were in shock and did not want to talk about it. I thought, *If I can't beat this cancer, Lord, then make it my friend, and help me to help my children understand that. Help them to understand that because of the cancer, I am going home to heaven to be with my Lord and my husband so very soon, where I belong."* The tears continued to stream down my face, almost creating a puddle on the floor. Mary then added, "Thank you for letting me talk to you about this. I can't explain this to my daughter. It would make her cry."

Oh dear, if she were to look over here right now and see me crying, I would have broken her trust that she could confide in me. I had to pull it together, but my heart was aching to think she was going to have to go through this without her children. I was going to have to really pray about this.

The nurse visits increased as Mary's cancer advanced. Her angel visits continued right along as before, but her exciting visions into heaven were just beginning. She had a lot to tell me when I came for my hospice visit. I knew her heart yearned to share it with her family, but I did not know how that was going to happen. I had been praying but still did not know what to do. When the visit ended, I reminded her that I would be on call tonight, that if she needed anything to just call and I would be up to see her. I leaned over the bed rail and kissed her on her forehead. She gave me that precious smile, and I was off.

That night around nine p.m., my pager went off. I called the hospital and was given a number to call. I called the number, and when they answered, I said, "Hi, this is the hospice nurse. How can I help you?"

The quiet female voice on the other end of the phone said, "You don't know me, but I am Gretchen, Mary's daughter, and I would like to know how she is doing."

I almost dropped the phone. Immediately I said a quick, frantic prayer. "God, I have to say something to her. You know I am going to say something, and that is against the rules. This is breaking patient confidentiality. I didn't ask Mary if I could discuss what she and I talked about with her daughter. I might only have this one chance to talk to her daughter. I have never met this lady. What if she gets mad at what I tell her? What if I yell at her for hurting her mother? What if she tells my boss? What if I get fired? What if Mary dies without family there? ... Lord, please, I need an answer and I need it now!"

After I collected my thoughts, I began to tell her that I was actually the nurse who had seen her mother today, and all things considered, she was doing as well as could be expected. Then Gretchen began to cry and tell me that she had decided not to go see her mother ever again because she could not bear to see her suffer, and she certainly could not be there when her mother was dying. She wanted to remember her the way she was. So, if it would be all right, could she call me weekly for a report on her mother? By this time, Gretchen was really crying and could hardly get the words out. I thought,

Okay, God, here we go. Please give me the right words. I asked Gretchen if she had a few minutes to talk to me. I told her I had a few things I wanted to discuss with her, and she agreed. I prayed, "God, please give me the right words that she needs to hear that will bring her back to her mom's side and be with her through the rest of this journey. Amen."

"What I am about to share with you, Gretchen, is what your mom and I talked about on several occasions during my hospice visits. I don't have your Mom's permission to share this, but knowing she so wanted you to have this information, I am going to take the chance that she will forgive me for telling you."

I started out by telling Gretchen that Mary had made peace with her cancer and she wanted her children to also. There was no cure for it, so they should make peace with it. The cancer was going to take her home soon to be with her Lord in heaven. She was going to also get to see her beloved husband, whom her broken heart never got over.

Gretchen sobbed at the other end of the phone as she said, "But I don't want to lose my mom."

I explained that it was not our choice. If she couldn't get well, we couldn't wish her to stay here. We had to let her go home with the Lord, where she had the promise of healing and eternal life. I added, "Staying away from your mother is not going to keep her here any longer. It is just going to make the short time she has left very sad."

Then I began to explain the beautiful visions of heaven she was beginning to see. I heard a gasp at the other end of the phone. I said, "Yes, as it reads in the Bible, 'Whenever anyone turns to the Lord, the veil is taken away.' The closer your mom gets to dying, the thinner the veil becomes, so her view will get more beautiful every day. People who have gone before her will come and visit with her. Actually, she has been visiting with someone every day lately. In fact, your grandmother was there again today."

There was a silence at the other end of the phone. I waited a few seconds and then asked, "Gretchen, are you all right?"

A little voice came back and said, "I think so."

I decided I had nothing to lose at this point so I might as well finish strong. "So Gretchen, if this was my mom, I would be right by her side for her final journey. That is the most-coveted spot to be in when your loved one is dying. You will be standing on hallowed ground when the Lord is ready and comes for your mom. The room will be filled with angels. You can just feel them like electricity in the room, and when you feel the brush of an angel wing, you know the Lord is in the room. It is an awesome feeling, and you need to experience with your mother. Gretchen, she wants her family right there with her more than anything. She told me. She knew you were afraid, so she didn't tell you how much it meant to her. She didn't want you to feel obligated. That is how moms are."

I thanked her for letting me talk to her and told her if she had any question to call any time. Gretchen was tearful but quiet when she said her good-byes. She had a lot to think about. I went to bed and prayed, "God, it is in your hands now."

I went to see Mary two days later for our regularly scheduled visit. When I got to the door, I heard some chatter coming from inside the room. When I pushed the door open farther, there was Mary in the bed, with someone sitting on the bed beside her and pictures scattered all over the place. These two were sharing old memories and making new ones. Mary was so glad to see me and couldn't wait to introduce me to her daughter.

The lady on the bed jumped up and stood in front of me as Mary said, "Jan, I would like to introduce you to my daughter, Gretchen."

We both smiled so big, and as I put my hand out to shake hers, she gave me a wink, wrapped her arms my neck, and squeezed me for what felt like an eternity.

Mary said, "Well it looks like you two know each other."

Gretchen said, "No, Mother, I just want to hug one of the nurses who have been taking such great care of you."

This by far was my favorite visit with Mary. When I

had finished with the visit, and I leaned over, kissed her on the forehead, and hugged her for what would be my last hug. Had I known, I would have held onto her for a little bit longer. Mary thanked me for everything, and then she winked. How did she know? When Gretchen walked me to the door, I asked her if she had told her mom we had talked. She said she had never mentioned our little visit. Some things will always remain a mystery.

Mary went home to be with the Lord a few days after my last visit. But all was well. She got to spend some good time with her daughter before she died, and little did she know that her daughter was going to walk her to the edge of heaven and hand her off to the Lord. Gretchen called me shortly after her mom passed away. Then through her tears she thanked me for not letting her continue to hurt her precious mom any more than she already had, and for not letting her miss her mom's final journey. Gretchen went on to tell me her mom had been seeing beautiful visions as she looked around, then would explain them to her with wide-eyed excitement each time she would see them. Then Gretchen became a little tearful when she mentioned conversations her mom was having with different people, including Gretchen's dad. Gretchen said her mom slept sound while she sat quietly beside her holding her hand. All at once, her eyes opened, she looked over at Gretchen and smiled, her hand went limp, and she was gone.

Gretchen started to cry, and I said, "Do you understand what you just did? You just walked your precious mother to the edge of heaven and handed her off to the Lord. You just stood on hallowed ground, Gretchen."

I heard small gasp on the other end of the phone. "You did it, Gretchen. You didn't only go see your mother; you walked her home. I am so proud of you, and you made your mom so happy."

Through her tears, Gretchen agreed she wouldn't have wanted to be anywhere else but right here in this very place right beside her mother, and to think she almost missed it. Gretchen said, "I want to thank you for talking me into being here for Mom's final journey."

I smiled and said, "It wasn't me at all. It was all God."

Enjoy heaven, Mary. You deserve the best. PS, take care of that little piece of my heart you took with you. See you soon.

Whenever anyone turn to the Lord, the veil is taken away. (2 Corinthians 3:16, New Women's Devotional Bible)

3

Jesus as an Old Guy

It was Friday, the long work week had ended, and to the best of everyone's knowledge, the patients were all tucked in. Medications, caregivers, linens, and personal care items had all been delivered or discussed during that day's visit. The patients and their families all knew who the hospice nurse on call was for the weekend, so if they needed anything or had any questions, they all knew who to call.

I was the hospice nurse on call that weekend, and I felt an odd sense of uneasiness when I thought about it. The only reason I could come up with for my uneasiness was the fact that one of the other nurses had a late admit, and I had not been able to meet him yet, which was never a good idea, and I knew that. Usually, if we have a new patient, the hospice nurse on call goes to see the new patient, so if she should get called there in an emergency, or in the night, she knows exactly how to get to the patient's home and get there quickly. Some roads were very tricky, off the beaten path, and very hard to find to say the least. You needed to find them in the daylight if you were going to have any chance at all of finding them at night, unless you were blessed and your patient lived in a town. If they lived in the mountains or woods and you get lost, good luck because your cell phone wouldn't work there. It made for some very interesting hospice calls. Oh, I forgot to tell you, to make matters worse, I am geographically challenged. But they knew that when they hired me.

Well, I decided to quit worrying about it and go on about my weekend. I brought the new patient's chart home with me, so I could at least read the history and become familiar with his diagnosis. I stopped at the grocery store and proceeded to load up my cart. I had three growing teenage boys who knew how to eat, so buying groceries was almost an everyday occurrence. Just as I began to check out, my pager went off, so I called the hospital while the checker kept checking my cartful of groceries. Just as my luck would have it, I was to call the new patient's family as quickly as I could. I hurriedly paid for my groceries and stepped outside to call the number the hospital had given me.

When the person at the other end picked up, there was a frantic, "Hello!"

I said, "Hi, this is the hospice nurse. I was told to call you."

The frantic voice said, "You have to come quick. My son is having a seizure, and it won't stop. It is different than before; you have to bring something to stop it!"

I assured the patient's mother I would be there as quickly as I possibly could. I explained I lived thirty miles away and had to call the doctor for an order and then find a pharmacy that was open to fill the order, but I would hurry as quickly as I could. Mom seemed less anxious when we hung up—maybe because she knew help was coming. Now if I could just find the patient's home.

I called my oldest son and explained he needed to meet me at the grocery store to pick up the groceries. I explained I had received a call and had to go out to see a patient. This was nothing new to my family. While I was waiting for my son, I took out the patient's chart, called his doctor, and informed her of the seizures. She prescribed a couple of medications for the patient for me to use to try to stop the seizures, and due to the late hour and the urgency of these medications, she agreed to meet me halfway to the patient's home with the prescriptions. While I was driving to meet the doctor, I called and begged a pharmacist at one of the local pharmacies to please stay open for me. I explained to the pharmacist that it was an emergency, and I was bringing the prescription from the doctor, who had agreed to meet me with them. The pharmacist agreed to wait. The local pharmacists knew all of us hospice nurses by name and dealt with us all on a daily basis. We all felt our local pharmacists were angels for going above and beyond to help us out when our hospice patients needed medications.

When I left the pharmacy, I had about ten miles to go. By this time, it was dark, the rain was pouring down, and the wind was blowing me all over the road. When I got into town, I took out the patient's chart and reread the address. I watched carefully so I didn't miss my turn. I finally found the street, turned off the highway, and began my adventure. I drove quite a distance off the main highway into a wooded area. I ended up in a large cookie-cutter subdivision where all the houses looked alike. I followed the map precisely, and when I stopped, it was not the street or the correct house. I backed out and drove up and down the streets looking for the street I needed. The wind and rain were making it difficult to see. My wipers were on high, and I was still having difficulty seeing. When I realized my cell phone did not work here, I decided to try to get back to the highway. But getting back to the highway proved to be impossible because I was lost in a sea of lookalike houses. I was staring to panic. I was lost and had the medications to stop my patient's seizures with me. All I could hear in my head was his mother's frantic voice telling me to come quickly and help her son. I had no way to call and ask for directions, nor had I even seen a car all night that I could stop to ask them for directions. No one but me would be out in this storm. There were probably flood warnings out, but that was the least of my worries right now. I finally stopped in the middle of the road and started to cry. I put my head on the steering wheel and began to pray.

"Lord, I am lost, and I am asking you please to help me. My patient is having seizures, he is suffering, and his mother is so worried about him, as you well know. Lord, the medicine he needs here in my car, and again, I can't get it to him without your help. I can't even find my way back to the highway. There is no cell phone service here, so I can't even call his family for directions. So Lord, I have no idea how you are going to fix this one. I just know you will. However, this time, Lord, you have to do it quickly because he needs this medicine."

Just then there was a knock on my passenger window. I raised my head off the steering wheel and opened the window without a moment's hesitation. There stood a nice old guy in a raincoat holding a little schnauzer.

He said, "Hi, young lady, can I help you?"

I said, "Yes, you sure can. I'm lost."

He said, "Where are you trying to go?"

After I read him the address, he said, "There is no street around here with that name. Who is it you're looking for?"

Again, I started to cry and said, "I am a nurse, and I'm trying to find my patient's home. Telling you the name would be a breach of privacy, so I can't tell you that."

The sweet old man smiled and said, "Oh, I understand. Well don't worry. It will all be fine. Are you ready for your directions?"

With a tearful grin, I said, "Yes, I guess so."

So he began. "Go straight to end of this road, make a left, and keep going. It will eventually turn into gravel, but don't worry, just keep going. You will come to a curve in the road. It will curve to the left. There you will drive out of the wooded area, and there will be some more houses. The fourth house on your left will have the yard light on, and there will be a man standing in the yard with a yellow rain slicker on. He is waiting for you. Good luck. Drive safe."

I quickly said good-bye and then realized I had not said thank you to this precious man. So I opened my car door and stepped out into the rain to tell him thank you, and to my surprise, there was no one out there. The street light shined bright above my car, but there was no old man and a little dog to be seen. I didn't have time to put much thought into it right then. I was too worried about my patient. I just jumped back in my car and followed the directions the sweet old man had just given me. Sure enough, when I came around the last bend, there was an opening in the trees, and at the fourth house on the left, the yard light was on. In the yard stood a man with a yellow rain slicker on waving at me.

I slowly pulled into the driveway, put down my window, and the man said, "You must be our hospice nurse."

I said, "Yes I am. I am so sorry for the delay. I got lost."

He said, "We should have made sure you had good directions, and we should have told you your cell phone would not work up here after you turn off the highway."

I said, "Well, I am here now. Let's go start this medication."

I finally got to my patient's home around 7:30 that night, and I left there around 3:30 the next morning. It took me that many hours and several calls to his physician to get the patient's seizures under control and the patient comfortable. When we tucked the patient into bed and I was ready to leave, the patient's father stood by the front door with his rain slicker and hat on.

I said, "Are you going somewhere at this hour?"

He said, "I am going to make sure our angel makes it back to the highway without any more trouble this visit."

So, I got a special escort back to the highway from this sweet, tired, worried father. Needless to say, I had a very special bond with this young patient and his family from day one until the very end. Of course, I had to endure some teasing about getting lost trying to find their beautiful woodsy dwelling, but this family was worth every minute of it.

As I left for home some eight hours later, I was going over the night in my head, just making sure I had done everything possible. Then I started going over my checklist of things the patient needed for the next day. When my day started in a few hours, I needed to order a hospital bed for this patient and get it delivered. I needed to deliver bedding for the hospital bed to the patient's home and get all his medications reordered. My mind was reeling as I approached the road where I turned off the highway the previous night and got lost. My mind instantly jumped back to the sweet old guy who gave me directions. I had completely forgotten about him. I had been too busy with being lost and a seizing patient to think about it until now. How did he give me such perfect directions when the address I gave him wasn't even an actual street, or the fact that I couldn't give him the patient's name? My mind whirled with questions. I pulled over onto the side of the road. How did I dare open my window to a perfect stranger? I would never have done that, ever. What was I thinking? Then I began to replay it all in my mind. I remembered right before the sweet old guy knocked on the passenger window, I was praying.

I said, "Lord, I am lost, and I am asking you please to help me. My patient is having seizures, he is suffering, and his mother is so worried about him, as you well know. Lord, I have the medicine he needs here in my car, and again, I can't get it to him without your help. I can't even find my way back to the highway. I have no cell service here, so I can't even call his family for directions. So, Lord, I have no idea how you are going to fix this one. I just know you will; however, this time, Lord, you have to do it quickly because he needs this medicine."

"Could this have really been Him?" I said with a grin. Yes, of course it was. I put my head down on the steering wheel and began to cry. I then began to pray.

"Lord, wow, that was you, wasn't it? You sent an angel down to show me the way, didn't you? You did it so quickly, just like I asked. The patient really needed his medication, Lord. Thank you. Oh, and thank you for being right there at the patient's home with us. I felt you. We couldn't have made it through the night without you. Please keep your strong arms wrapped around that young patient and his family, Lord. They are scared and facing more challenges throughout this short journey, and I will keep praying. One last thing, Lord. Please tell your angel thank you from me. He left before I could thank him and his little dog. As always, thank you, Lord. I love you."

When I arrived at home, I got out my Bible and looked up scriptures to see if I could prove what just happened to me that night. I knew what happened and who it was, but I always wanted to be ready if someone challenged me, and sure enough here is what I found:

For He will command His angels concerning you to guard you in all your ways. (Psalm 91:11 NIV)

Do not neglect to show hospitality to strangers, for thereby some have entertained angels unawares. (Hebrews 13:2 ESV)

Do not forget to show hospitality to strangers, for by so doing some people have shown hospitality to angels without knowing it. (Hebrews 13:2 NIV)

And my God will meet All your needs according to the riches of His glory in Christ Jesus. (Philippians 4:9 NIV)

For we walk by faith, not by sight. (2 Corinthians 5:7 NKJV)

I knew it. There it was, to name just a few. He is always right there if we need Him. For some reason, God was going to make sure I knew He could always be trusted to be there, especially in this job. What was it about this job? I wasn't only learning to not fear death, but I was learning so much about my own faith.

Monday morning arrived, and it always starts out with weekend report from the on-call nurse reporting on any patients that she saw over the weekend and their updated condition. Well this Monday report was just a little bit different. It started with Jan reporting, "I just may have met Jesus this weekend ..."

4

Is Anyone Going to Answer the Phone?

"Hello, Margaret! Hello," I yelled as she lumbered by, pushing the lawnmower. I was waving franticly, trying to get her attention so I could stop her before she fell in the yard. I didn't know who was letting this elderly lady still mow her lawn, but it had to stop. She was going to get hurt. Finally, she saw me and stopped the mower.

"Well hello there," she said. "I didn't remember you were coming today. Let's go in the house. I need a break anyway."

I smiled and tried to answer her, but she did not hear me, which did not surprise me, because I had read in her chart where it said she was nearly deaf. So I just hurried in behind her, anxious to meet her for the first time.

Margaret and I sat down in the living room, and I

introduced myself, very loudly, of course. I found that if I spoke clearly and loudly and looked directly at her, she could hear me without much trouble at all. We chatted a while to get to know each other, and I found out she was just as cute as she could be. I knew before long into our first conversation that she had already found her way right into my heart. Now it was time for business. We had to do Ms. Margaret's assessment, and when we were done, Margaret was pleased to know she was doing just fine today.

When I had finished her assessment, I had every intention of discussing with her the fact that I did not want her mowing the lawn anymore. I was going to explain my reasoning was that at her age, and the fact that she was really very ill (even though at the present time she was feeling great), she could fall and get seriously hurt.

But before I could say a thing, Margaret looked over the top of her glasses at me, raised one finger, and said, "I think you and I are going to get along just fine because you didn't come in here trying to tell me what I can and can't do. I told my kids, just because some doctor says I am dying and that I must go on hospice does not mean I am going to quit doing things for myself. I will quit when *I* think it is time to quit."

I smiled, swallowed hard, and agreed with her, as if the thought had never ever crossed my mind. Nursing

101—know how to pick your battles, and know the ones you have already lost.

Margaret's cancer was out of remission, and the doctors did not give her much time. The doctor suggested the family get her signed onto hospice right away and not wait until she was bedbound. Now as you can tell, Margaret was one very independent lady. Her children sided with the doctor and insisted she get admitted to hospice so they knew someone was keeping an eye on her at least a couple of times a week. But even with hospice in the picture, Margaret was going to be in charge if she possibly could. Margaret had six of the most loving children ever. She had four girls and two boys who loved their mother with all their hearts and would do anything for her—that is if she would let them. She was fiercely independent and always had been.

The next week when I made my visit, I noticed the neighbor boy was mowing Margaret's lawn. When I asked her about it, she just grumbled something about her children always interfering with her business. "They don't think I can do anything!"

I never said another thing about it, wishing I had never brought that up. I moved quickly onto a lighter subject, and soon we were laughing and talking. I just loved visiting with her. She was such a feisty little old lady, and I wanted to be just like her one day. As we sat there chatting, all relaxed, out of nowhere, an alarm went off. A real fire alarm, the gold, round metal thing that the little hammer bangs against. It is usually on the outside of the fire house wall on purpose so you can hear it a great distance away. Oh, but not this one. It was on the living room wall, which was directly behind me. Talk about losing five years of my life. I let out a scream and jumped up, not sure what to do, where to go, or how to get Margaret out if it really was a fire. What was this awful noise, and how would we stop it? I finally looked over at Margaret, and she was watching all my commotion with a smile on her face.

She said, "That is just my telephone, dear."

Only I couldn't hear her. I just had to read her lips because if felt like my ears were bleeding. Sure enough, the dreadful ringing stopped as soon as she picked up the receiver of her phone. Was this the ringer on her phone? Should that not have been *written in red* on the front of her chart? The admit nurse and I were going to have a chat, maybe in sign language if I still couldn't hear by the time I got back to work.

Margaret was sitting on the couch chatting quite loudly to one of her daughters. Her son had fixed the speaker on her phone so the volume was turned way up, so that their mom could hear the caller talking. It worked great. However, everyone else in the room got in on their conversation, whether they wanted to or not. Not only did her boys rig up the ringer so she and all of town could hear her phone ringing, but now anyone in her house could hear her conversation. I was just glad I could hear them talking. I thought after that fire alarm, I would never hear again. I just sat there quietly finishing my charting while Margaret finished her conversation with her daughter.

When she was ready to hang up, she said, "It was nice you called, Steve. Tell your wife and the kids hi from me."

I could hear her daughter yelling, "Mom, no, it's me, Janet, and this isn't Steve."

Margaret hung up the phone and said, "That was my son, Steve, and he calls all the time."

I just smiled. I wasn't sure if I should correct her or not. If I was the daughter, I would have wanted credit for that wonderful phone call, but was this another one of those Nursing 101 no-win things? I had to think about it.

Margaret's health continued downhill quickly, just as the doctor had predicted. She went from up walking around doing her own things to bedbound in a matter of days. Even though I knew this was coming, it didn't make it any easier. The hospice nurses have a process of letting go too, and this nurse wasn't any more ready to let her go than the family was. You just learn to pull it together and get ready, because there is one very special family there that belongs to that very special patient who needs his or her nurse to have it all together—to walk with them through their loved one's final journey, and to gently weave them in and out of their grieving process enough for them to understand that they are standing on hallowed ground every moment they are in her room. They truly are in the coveted spot. There are some who only get to dream of being there when their loved one is dying. If you are very lucky, you get to not only be there but walk your loved one to the edge of heaven and hand him or her off to the Lord when it is time. When you have managed to get a family into this frame of mind, usually there is no turning back for them. They are beside the patient until the end. As the nurse, I just continue to pray, and let God finish what He started. Without Him by my side all the way through every visit, I am not sure I'm a strong enough person to do any of this, so this is all God. I am just His coworker, His fingerprints, if you will. I only follow His lead.

Margaret had been comfortably drifting in and out of sleep for a few hours now. She was getting very close. On her last assessment, I told the family she was declining quite rapidly now, and it wouldn't be long. I told them she was very comfortable, and that was truly a blessing from God. All the daughters and daughters-in-law were snuggled around her bed, taking turns holding her hands and telling fun stories of their childhood memories. I was so wishing Margaret wasn't so deaf. The men were all out in the living room watching sports but would nervously wander in and out of the bedroom occasionally to check on Margaret. All the grandchildren who could not be here and other close relatives had called and said their good-byes to Margaret yesterday when she was more awake. Oh and by the way, the fire alarm phone ringer had been disconnected. It was just a normal little ring out in the living room when a call came in, and it was barely audible from Margaret's room. Thank goodness.

I was standing quietly at the end of the bed charting, while the girls were still chattering like before, and Margaret was sound asleep. Now unbeknownst to us, all of the men, for whatever reason, had stepped outside. Just then the telephone started to ring in the living room. It was such a tiny little ring that I had to strain to even tell it was a ring. The girls didn't even hear it at first. It rang a second time, then a third time, and then it rang a fourth time.

After the fourth ring, Margaret opened her eyes and said, "Is anybody going to answer that phone?"

Everyone looked around in sheer amazement and laughed. One of the daughters said, "Mom, can you hear that?"

Margaret grumbled, "Of course I can hear it. It just woke me up."

There was not a dry eye in the room. The girls were excitedly asking their mom if she had been listening to their stories. Margaret just smiled and admitted she had been listening and was loving it.

I said, "Margaret, how do you like that? God started

healing you on this side of heaven. You got your hearing back."

She just smiled. Then the men were all called in so they could get in on God's miracle and talk with Ms. Margaret awhile before she fell asleep.

Before long, Ms. Margaret went home to be with the Lord, and there was no doubt in anyone's mind that Margaret heard all their good-byes and their "I love you, Moms" because God made sure that family got in on that little miracle before He took her home. I also made sure Margaret's children knew that they had just walked their precious Mother to the edge of heaven and handed her off to the Lord. They were standing on hallowed ground because the Lord had just been in this room when He came to get her. Margaret's children smiled through their tears as they hugged one another. There was a peace throughout the room with all of Margaret's children, and that was thanks to God.

As I was driving home, I prayed and thanked God for the peace He poured out over Margaret's family. The closure the family received by getting to talk to their mother and knowing she heard their stories and good-byes before she died was huge for her and the kids. Thank you for always providing what we need. As it says in the Bible, you promise to always provide all our needs.

Now I have a question. Does healing always start on this side of heaven, God?

5

Have You Read the Newspaper This Morning?

Beginning my day with Maudie was always a perfect was to start any day. I arrived at 8:30 a.m. for my scheduled appointment. "Right on time. Come on in," Barb announced as she swung the kitchen door open. Barb continued, "I'm just finishing breakfast dishes. We are so slow this morning. I haven't even read mom the paper yet. Why don't you just go on in and visit with her? I will be in after a little while to join you two." So, I agreed and made my way into the living room, where Maudie's hospital bed was set up.

Maudie was a cute, feisty little ninety-year-old who could hold her own. Just visiting with Maudie made it hard to remember that she was dying from a devastating disease, but she was and never once complained about it.

She lived with her daughter Barb, who took wonderful care of her mom. Barb and Maudie had quite a routine. Barb would read the newspaper cover to cover to Ms. Maudie every morning after breakfast because Maudie had to keep up on the news. Barb was reading the newspaper to Maudie because she had gone completely blind several years ago. The two of them were very close, and Barb was sure going to miss her when she was gone.

Meanwhile Maudie was sitting up in bed when I walked into the room with the bedside table in front of her and the newspaper lying on top of the table. I greeted Ms. Maudie as I came into the room.

With an impish grin on her face, she said, "Good morning, Jan. I have been waiting for you. How is your day so far? Mine has been amazing."

I stood beside her bed, looking at her with a little suspicion, wondering what was up. Then finally curiosity got the best of me, and I asked her to explain what made it so amazing.

Maudie said, "Come closer. I have to tell you something." I leaned over the bed so I was right in next to Maudie, and then she whispered, "I read the paper myself today!"

I stepped back and looked at her as she sat there smiling at me. She challenged me, "Should I read some of the paper to you?" I was still unable to speak. I just shook my head yes as Maudie quietly began to read the headlines of the newspaper word for word and then continued down the page to other interesting topics.

I looked at her with tears in my eyes and said, "Maudie, it's a miracle. Have you told your daughter?"

Maudie said, "Shhhh, no, I was waiting for you to get here so you could tell her. She won't believe me."

I laughed and said, "Just read the paper to her."

Maudie smiled, and her eyes twinkled with only a twinkle God could have put there. I asked Maudie when she first noticed she could see. Maudie replied, "When I woke up this morning and looked around at everything in this room, I thought I had died and went to heaven because you are healed in heaven. Then I realized I was still in my bed and this must be my daughter's house. What do you think, Jan?" Before I could answer, we heard Barb coming from the kitchen. Maudie leaned back on the bed as if nothing had changed.

When Barb walked into the living room, she asked how I thought Maudie was doing today. I told her I thought she was doing better than ever and that Maudie had something she wanted to tell Barb. Barb looked first at Maudie and then back at me. Maudie slowly picked up the newspaper and began to read the headlines of the paper. Barb's hand softly covered her mouth, and tears rolled down her cheeks as Maudie continued to read aloud from the newspaper.

When Maudie stopped reading, Barb asked, "Mother,

when did this happen? When did you get your eyesight back? Jan, what does this mean?"

Maudie smiled and with a tear replied, "When I woke up this morning, I could see. I didn't know what it meant, so I kept quiet. I just studied your beautiful face at breakfast, Barb, so I will always have that etched in my memory if my sight should go as fast as it returned. I didn't want to get your hopes up. I wanted to ask Jan what she thought first."

As tears ran down Barb's face, she hugged Maudie tight as if it was their last hug. When they finished, they were ready for an answer, and I was praying for the Lord to speak through me as I always did, because I did not have an answer for this patient and family.

Ever since I started at hospice, I have been assuring families that in Revelation, God promises that their loved ones will be healed once they get to heaven.

As Maudie and Barb laughed, I explained my point here was that I thought when patients were very close to the end of their journey, our loving God would start healing the patient on this side of heaven. These were only my thoughts from watching this happen a few times over the years. I wished God were there for me to ask.

Maudie replied, "I think that makes perfect sense to me, and we do serve a loving God, that is for sure." Then with a look of seriousness, she asked, "Do you think I am that close to going home?"

I had just completed Maudie's assessment for this visit and replied, "Your vital signs are stable as usual, and your skin is warm and pink. You are weak and your appetite is poor, which is no change, but you know only God has the real answer to your question, Ms. Maudie."

Maudie smiled. She was looking forward to going to heaven. She always said at ninety she deserved to get out of this old world and meet her loving Savior. As I finished up today's visit, I gave them both a big hug and told them to enjoy the miracle from God today.

After I left, I pondered over Maudie's miracle the rest of the day as I continued seeing all my patients. I finished my paperwork and went home to a nice quiet night of no "on call," which was rare but very welcome. The evening was quiet, and I had a chance to get to bed early. As I knelt beside my bed to journal my prayers, as I do most nights, I knew this would take a while. I had a lot to pray about tonight. When I journal, I always include a prayer for my hospice patients, and tonight was no different, Maudie was at the forefront of my mind. I started to journal, and as I got to my hospice patients, I started asking God about Maudie. Just then my cell phone on the nightstand started to ring. I answered it, thinking it was one of my boys. On the other end of the phone was Barb.

She was crying and finally could say, "Jan, I am so sorry to bother you. I know you are not on call, but I wanted to tell you Mom is gone. We were watching TV together, I was holding her hand, and suddenly, her hand went limp in mine. I looked over and she was gone. She did get her eyesight back just before she went home to heaven."

I just sat there. I did not know what to say. This family needed me, and I had no words. I finally said, "Barb, I am so sorry for your loss. I did not see this coming. She had no signs of imminent death this morning when I completed her assessment. However, I will say God does keep me and other hospice nurses alike humble this way. Even when we can see the obvious signs of imminent death and can get close to the amount of time a patient has left when the family asks, we are always reminded by times like this that the time when a patient dies is always in God's perfect timing, not anyone else's."

Barb said, "I know Mom was ready to go, but it was just such a shock. I am going to miss her so much, but I am so happy she is not bedridden anymore. She is free."

Following the phone call, after I collected my thoughts, I went back to my journal and explained to God I had no idea where to start writing. Ever since I have started this hospice journey with my patients, the Lord has shown me so much about death that I never knew before, and I guess I am still learning every day. The most important thing I learned is that death is not scary or to be feared at all. It is the most peaceful and serene you can be on this side of heaven.

Lord, I want to thank you for leading me on this path in life and allowing me to be your fingerprints on our patients. Thank you for never leaving my side.

He will wipe every tear from their eyes. There will be no more death' or mourning or crying or pain, for the old order of things has passed away. (Revelation 21:4 NIV)

6

The Curmudgeon

In all my years as a hospice nurse, only one thread wove all my hospice visits together, and that was God. Each patient and his or her journey was as different as night and day. I don't think there were two alike in all my eleven years. With each new admit came a new adventure, and this admit was no different.

You see, Joe, the new admit, was a curmudgeon. The joke in the office was to send me out to see all the crabby old men for their first couple of hospice visits until I had them all sweetened up. For some unknown reason, I had a quite a knack for getting along with those crabby old men.

While going over Joe's chart, familiarizing myself with Joe's diagnosis and history, I did learn that Joe did not believe in God. This was going to be a challenge, but we were used to that. You see, with hospice we were instructed to meet all our patients wherever they were spiritually, without pushing any of our religious beliefs on them. With people like Joe, I would not be able to bring up religion at all. The patient must bring it up and want to talk about it. I knew from what I read that was not going to be the case, so I would just go to the Lord in prayer for Joe every day. I prayed and asked for help talking to Joe about the Lord.

On my first trip out to see Joe, I prayed for God to give me the right words and to stay on Joe's good side if possible. Before I got to the door, I reached up and put my cross necklace inside the collar of my shirt so at least that did not offend him right away. I knocked, and Joe answered the door. I saw quickly that my boss was right: he was crabby. I introduced myself as I entered the kitchen.

Joe growled, "I'm Joe. You can have a seat at the table." Joe then continued, "I want to get a few things straight. There will be no talk about God in this house. I don't want a bunch of different nurses rummaging around in here in my things. I don't want to talk about my dying. You discuss everything with me and not my nosy family. I have no children. They all are my nieces and nephews. They mean well, but they are all about to drive me crazy with their church and God talk. So, I don't need any nurse doing the same thing. Did you hear me?"

I swallowed hard and said, "Of course I heard you.

We will always respect all your wishes, Joe. I can't say I will be your only hospice nurse, but I will come as often as I can."

It seemed like after we got that out of the way, I made a lot of small talk, figuring out what areas were land mines and should be left undiscussed and which areas were safe. By the end of what felt like a very long visit, we were conversing like he was going to tolerate me. I completed a quick assessment of his vital signs and explained I would visit again in a couple of days. Joe made sure it was going to be me, as he reminded me again he didn't want a bunch of strangers rummaging through his house all the time. I assured him it would be me.

I continued to go see Joe for the next couple of weeks. Joe grew to trust me. We were like old friends. We talked about anything and everything during our visits. I think he began to enjoy them even though he would never admit it. Joe told me during one of our visits that his wife of fifty years had died almost two years ago, and he was missing her terribly. He would get tearful just mentioning her.

Eventually I learned the one subject I would run scared from is when Joe brought up his family coming over trying to get him to go to church with them. He would start this long rant. Everyone in his family, including his beloved late wife, believed in God and they thought he should too, and that made him so angry. I always knew when his family had been over the night before, or earlier in the day before I got there, because I got the fallout from it. I wanted to tell the family that their fire-and-brimstone approach was only making the hospice nurses cannon fodder, but I didn't. I just prayed and asked God for more help with Joe. I prayed God would show me how to help Joe find his way. I wanted so badly for Joe to go to heaven and to be with his wife, but Joe was the most stubborn man I had ever run across.

As our visits continued, Joe and I became so very close that at times I forgot my promise not to talk about God.

One day as Joe was telling me a story about his wife, he became tearful and said, "The pain of never seeing her again is almost unbearable."

Without even thinking, I said, "What makes you so sure you are never going to see her again?"

I swallowed hard, realizing what I had just said. Joe looked up at me with tears still in his eyes. He said, "My wife was a beautiful, godly women, and there is no doubt in my mind that she went straight to heaven when she died, but I am not good enough to go to heaven, nor will I ever be, so I don't ever want to talk about this again."

Oh, I had crossed the line. Would Joe ever trust me again? Had I ruined our friendship?

I prayed as I drove home. My heart was aching. "Lord, what have I done? I have broken my promise to my very special friend. Is he ever going to trust me again? Lord, he is confiding his deepest heartache to me, and all I can do is listen and pray to myself. Lord, he needs a minister in here to lead him to you, not a hospice nurse, but he won't allow that, so Lord, I am praying for a miracle."

By the next visit, Joe obviously forgave me, because him being angry at me was never mentioned again. We stayed as close as we were, but I never crossed that line during our visits again. I did, however, pray even more than I had before for Joe. I prayed God would please help Joe find his way, and if I could help, that He would show me what to do.

Before long Joe's cancer progressed, and he became bedbound. His family was taking turns staying with him and providing for him. They wanted so badly to provide for his spiritual needs as well but were to afraid. They knew how angry the subject of God and heaven previously had made him. If they forced the issue anymore, they were afraid he would throw them all out of his house and hire agency caregivers, and they would not see him again before he died. So the family prayed quietly for him in the other rooms out of sight, and then when Joe was sound asleep, they would pray over him. Speaking of praying for him, I was told that one of Joe's nephews could pray aloud so beautifully it was like he was one of God's very own angels. I never heard what nephew it was, but the next time I prayed I asked God if possible and it worked into his plan for Joe, could I please hear Joe's nephew pray.

I was beginning to lose hope that Joe was going to listen to anyone about God. I had even been letting my cross show for several visits now so Joe knew where I stood about being a Christian. I was so hoping he would ask me some questions about it, but he didn't, and I will admit I was too afraid to bring it up knowing how he reacted to the subject before when his family brought it up. Was I afraid, or did I just respect Joe's wishes? Joe and I had become good friends, and I didn't want to take the chance of forcing something on him now when he was lying in bed so sick. I had made him a promise not to talk about God with him in his home. I continued to pray for God to show me what to do, and to give me the right words to say. I was so afraid I was running out of time.

The next day Joe had another marked decline. His nursing visits went from three times a week to daily overnight. There was a nurse in to see him every day that week. His eating had slowed to a stop, and he was tolerating only a few sips of water a day by the end of the week. Joe was declining rapidly before my eyes.

The next day was Friday. I had a full day of patients to see up north, plus it was my weekend on call. For instance, the nurse on call would usually see the patient or patients that were the nearest to the end of their journey on that Friday so she could assess those patients herself. The nurse would make sure the patients and their families had everything they could possibly need, and also so that the families were aware of what nurse to call over the weekend if they should need one.

Joe was our sickest patient at the time, so on my way north to see my day's worth of patients, I stopped in to see him. He was getting so weak that he was sleeping most of the time now.

But when I whispered, "Good morning, Joe," he opened his beautiful brown eyes and gave me that sweet smile that I was used to seeing now.

He reached for my hand and whispered, "Good morning, Jan."

I asked him how he was doing, and of course he answered, "I've never been better," and everyone in the room laughed. Now did I mention how much I had grown to love this man? That was my downfall in this job. I dearly loved every one of my patients, and they knew it. No matter how hard I tried to keep it strictly professional on my part, I would end up loving every one of them in their own way. I treated them all as if they were my very own flesh and blood, or how I would want someone to treat my parents. I believe that is what God would have wanted me to do if He Himself would have left me a book of instructions on *How to Care for My Children.*

I did a full assessment on Joe and saw there were no changes from the day before. I informed him and his family that I was going north to see patients all day and that I would be stopping in again to see them this afternoon on my way back to the office. I reminded them that if they should need me before that for any reason, just call the number I had given them. They agreed, and Joe squeezed my hand and he whispered, "Good-bye" in his weak voice.

The day seemed unusually endless. Every time my phone rang, my heart raced, expecting each call to be from Joe's family telling me he had passed. This was going to be a hard death for me. I was not ready for it. I had grown so close to this patient, he was one of the sweetest, kindest little old men I had ever met. I was so confused about how someone this sweet and kind could refuse to go to church with his wife or think he was not good enough to ever get to heaven. My heart ached when I remembered the time he confided in me that the thought of never seeing his wife again was unbearable. I so wanted Joe to let the Lord into his heart. Where was God? He was being so quiet. This death was going to be so hard on me.

It was a long drive from up north back to Joe's house, but that was a good thing, because I needed that time to pray. This had been a very long and stressful day, and I really needed to just go home and recharge, but I had one very important stop left to make. When I arrived at Joe's home, there was a man sitting in a chair beside Joe's bed with his head bowed praying. There was a lot of family in the kitchen talking, and cooking it looked like. They turned to say hello as I passed by, then went on with their discussion.

When I got beside the bed, I quietly said, "Hello, Joe."

He opened his eyes, gave me a smile, and said with a weak voice, "Jan, you came back."

I smiled and replied, "Of course I came back. I told you I was stopping back to check on you on my way home today."

By this time, the man who was praying had heard us talking and was up standing by the bed. He was sweet. He introduced himself as one of Joe's nephew's and was very concerned about how Joe was doing. I told him I was about to complete my assessment, and we would see. Joe seemed to be very fond of this nephew and seemed to be at ease with him staying in the room.

After my assessment, I noted Joe's vital signs had significantly decreased: his extremities were cool to the touch, his skin was now a dusky color, and his respirations had slowed. All the hallmark signs of impending death were present. I leaned on the rail of the bed, took Joe's hand, and said, "Joe, I see a marked decline from this morning's visit. Are you having any pain? Are you anxious about anything? Tell me, how are you feeling, my friend?"

He said, "I knew that. I don't have long left now." The nephew quickly turned away from the bed and broke into tears.

While I still had hold of Joe's hand, I said very bravely,

"Joe, is everything okay? Do you need anything from me? Do you need to talk to me about anything, or do you need to see anyone?"

I meant anyone like a minister but was afraid to come right out and say it. I was still respecting his wishes not to talk about God and religion. Joe smiled as if he knew I was squirming and said, "No, Jan, I'm fine."

With tears in my eyes, I kissed his forehead and told him I loved him and to have his family call me if he should need me. He nodded his head, squeezed my hand, and fell asleep.

The nephew was back up to the side of the bed as I gathered up my things and headed to the door. I told him good-bye and to be sure to call me if they needed anything. I headed to the front door, only to find it would not open. No matter what I did, the door would not open. It was as if I were locked in, but the door was not locked. I had always used this same door, and never had I ever had trouble opening it before. So I put my nursing bag and keys on the floor to free up both hands, but the door was not opening. Then it hit me! God did not intend for me to leave just yet.

I muttered under my breath, "God is this you? No, I am not going back in there. I did all I can do. I asked him if there was anything he wanted to talk about. He made me promise I would not talk about you. You have had all this time to soften his heart. I can't betray his confidence on his deathbed."

I began trying the door again, but it would not open. I looked around. It was as if time had stood still. No one was noticing I was having trouble with the door. Was I in the *Twilight Zone* or something? I said, "All right, all right, I will go back in there."

When I walked back into the living room where Joe's bed was, the nephew who was praying beside the bed acted as if I had never left. I reached over the bed and softly rubbed Joe's cheek with the back of my hand.

He opened his eyes and said, "Oh, hi, Jan, you're still here."

I said, "Yes, Joe, I am." As I put my hand down on Joe's chest over his heart, I said, "Joe, I need to know if everything is okay in here."

Joe reached up and held my hand on his chest and said, "Yes, Jan, of course it is," as he fell back to sleep.

I slid my hand out from under his, kissed his forehead, whispered I love you, and grabbed my nurse's bag. I said good-bye to the man at the bed and headed for the front door. Again, I pressed on the handle of the front door, and the door would not open. I pushed again and again. I kicked on the bottom of the door, and it would not open. I looked around, and no one seemed to even notice I could not get this door open.

I dropped my bag on the floor and said, "Okay, God,

what do you want from me this time? I already went back in there to Joe once. You heard him. He said everything is okay in his heart. I am not going to cross the line with him. I promised him. You can fix anything. You are God. I have prayed the entire time he has been my patient for you to soften his heart and bring him into your flock. I can't do anymore!"

So there I stood crying in the hallway and having this argument with God. Who did I think was going to win this one? When I looked around, it was like time again had stood still. Everyone had gone about what they were doing. No one had even noticed the crazy nurse was unable to make this door open and was having an argument with no one in the hallway. I tried one more time, and it still would not open no matter what I did to it.

I picked up my nurse's bag and said, "What do you want from me God?"

I drug my bag back into the living room, where Joe's bed was. I tossed my bag on the couch behind me and leaned on the bedrail, wondering what I was going to do. The man on the other side of the bed did not even say, "Hey, crazy lady. What is up with you?" He acted like it was perfectly normal for someone to come back in a second time.

Eventually I leaned over the rail of the bed and again took one of Joe's hands. He opened his beautiful brown eyes, gave me that smile that melted my heart, and said with a weak voice, "Jan, you're back."

Little did I know that was the last time I would get to see that face, on this side of heaven. I said, "Yes, I had to come back. I have something I want to ask you, Joe."

Joe opened his eyes and looked at me with a hint of curiosity and said, "What would that be, Jan?"

Fighting back tears, I held Joe's hand in mine and asked, "Joe, I want to know if it would it be all right if I asked your nephew to pray aloud for us before I leave today."

My heart was pounding, and my eyes were filled with tears. Joe said, "Sure, Jan, that would be nice."

I wanted to just sing I was so happy, and when I looked up at the nephew standing across the bed from me, his mouth was hanging wide open, and his eyes were as big as saucers. I folded my fingers into Joe's and folded my other hand over the top. I wanted to keep squeezing so I knew he was awake to hear every word of that prayer. I was sure hoping this was the nephew who had the ability to pray aloud and was not too shy now that we got a yes from Joe. I looked up at the nephew, who was still in shock, and I asked if he would please say a prayer.

He said, "I would love to more than you could ever know."

I closed my eyes and laid my cheek on Joe's fingers laced in mine as the nephew began to pray. That had to be the most beautiful prayer I had ever heard in my life. I kept squeezing Joe's hand, and every time I looked up at Joe, he had a beautiful smile on his face. When the prayer ended, I again kissed Joe on the forehead and assured him that I was leaving for sure this time. He kissed the top of my hand and whispered, "Thank you, Jan," and off to sleep he went. I thanked Joe's nephew for the most beautiful payer I had ever heard in my life.

Then before I left, I made sure the nephew had my numbers in case he needed to call me to come back out. I told him Joe was getting very close to the end and asked if he wanted me to stay. The nephew assured me he would be fine. I instructed him that when patients get close to the end of their journey and they are looking toward the Lord, he thins the veil so they can look straight into heaven, and some patients like to share their visions with family standing at the bedside. I did not want that to startle Joe's nephew. He assured me that it would not startle him. I then mentioned that when patients are nearing the end, loved ones that who gone on before them sometimes come back to see them before the Lord comes to get them. The nephew had a serious look on his face.

I said, "You won't see them. You will just hear Joe talking to them." Then the nephew smiled. I asked the nephew if he would do me a favor. He said sure. I asked, "If Joe wakes up before he passes on, will you please ask him if he has seen his wife for me?" With a little hesitation, the nephew agreed.

My phone rang a few hours after I got home. It was Joe's nephew informing me that Joe had just taken his last breath. My eyes welled with tears when I asked if he went peacefully. The nephew was very tearful as he told me about the death. He stated, "Joe woke up and spoke a few minutes right before he closed his eyes and was gone. I asked Joe if he had seen his wife like you asked me to do."

I held my breath a moment before I asked, "Well, what did he say?"

The nephew replied, "He said, 'Yes, I have. She was just here. She is waiting for me to come home.' Then closed his eyes and was gone, with a beautiful smile on his face."

I said to the nephew, "You did a wonderful job. You just walked your uncle Joe to the edge of heaven and handed him off to the Lord. I am going to pray and thank God right now for putting you at your uncle's bedside tonight. I can't think of anyone who could have done a better job. Thank you for taking such good care of my Joe."

I heard the nephew crying at the other end of the phone. I offered to come out immediately. The nephew declined, stating the rest of the family was there, and they were all going to pray and reminisce for a little while before the mortuary arrived. I reminded the nephew again to call if he or the family needed me for anything at all, that I would be right out.

You made it, Joe. How is heaven?

Prayer is the portal that brings the power of heaven down to earth, and after that phone call, I knew I had some praying to do myself. Lord, help me to always trust you and follow your lead. Help me to hear your voice. I only want what is best for all your children. I want my patients to see your love and joy shine through me onto them and your fingerprints all over my care for them. Thank you for never leaving me.

Be still and know that I am God. (Psalm 46:10 NIV)

7

You're Not Going to Believe Who I Just Talked To

My friends, I would like you to meet Ellen. From the very first moment I was introduced to her, I knew I had met someone very special. Ellen was a feisty seventy-nine-year-old who was living out every day to the fullest. Most days you would never know she was involved in the battle of her life against the end stages of a devastating cancer that was cutting her life short. Ellen wasn't one to complain much, and most days she wore the most beautiful smile you have ever seen. Due to her illness, Ellen was living with her daughter Anna and her family. Ellen knew her time was short, so she was making the most out of every moment she had.

While the grandchildren were at school and her daughter was at work, Ellen would try to keep her days busy while she was still independent. Ellen enjoyed reading, crocheting blankets, taking short walks around the neighborhood, and occasionally cooking when she felt up to it. Often Ellen's friend would stop by to visit her and to reminisce about old times once more, but usually that turned into a lot of tears and tissues. However, Ellen was so uplifting and positive to be around that she would end up comforting her friends more than they comforted her. They would all leave with as big of a smile as hers. Ellen's positive outlook came from loving the Lord. She was a good Christian, and it showed in everything that she did. That was our Ellen, one of God's very own, and I was so blessed to get to know her.

While Ellen was still having good days, our hospice visits were only scheduled for once or twice a week or as needed to monitor her vital signs and control her symptoms. I always looked forward to these visits because Ellen was such a joy to talk with. During one of our visits, Ellen shared that she had lost her husband suddenly about eighteen months earlier and that she missed him terribly every day. It was the first time I had to witness a sad look on her face, but before I could even comfort her, a smile slowly returned as she announced it was okay because he was waiting for her in heaven. Ellen was one of a kind. Her faith knew no bounds. She went on to tell me that she and her husband had four children, three girls and one boy, and it made her face light up to talk about them. She went on to elaborate that she was living with her oldest daughter, Anna, her husband, and their family. Then came her son, Jeff, who lived in a neighboring city, and finally her youngest daughter, Sarah, who lived several states away and flew in as often as she could to see her mom, but never often enough, according to Ellen. Once again, I noticed a sadness come over Ellen, this time as if she could cry. I could even see the pain deep in her eyes as she sat there with her hands in her lap staring off into the room. As I sat quietly, the thought crossed my mind that was only three children she mentioned, and she said they had four. In an instant, she was back from her deep thoughts and was sporting a little smile, but you could tell there was still a little sadness in her eyes. It was time to say my farewells for today's visit, and I assured her a hospice nurse would be back in a couple of days unless she needed one before that. I gave her an extra-long hug before I left and told her how much I loved her as she flashed me that beautiful smile.

We continued our regular twice-a-week visits, watching Ellen continually decline but never complain. She was the perfect patient. We watched her go from walking independently, to a walker, then to a wheelchair, and finally to bedbound in just two short months all while keeping her positive attitude. She was amazing. Ellen now was beginning to sleep more of the day. She was getting weaker each visit. We tried everything we could possibly think of to increase her appetite, but she just did not want to eat.

She would tell us, "You girls stop worrying about me. I'm just not hungry at all. I will eat when I'm hungry."

And she was right, and us hospice nurses knew it. That was all a part of God's perfect plan. When a patient begins to shut down, that is usually one of the first visuals we get is your body doesn't want food anymore. It is like your body doesn't remember what to do with it, but what God did was make the patient not hungry anymore. They have no cravings and are not thirsty. They are just satisfied. It is just the hospice nurses and families who must remember and stop trying to feed them when the patient says no.

Ellen's hospice visits increased to three times a week as she continued her steady decline. She always remained positive and fun to visit with, but this visit was different.

When my assessment was over and I had explained to Ms. Ellen exactly how she was doing today, Ellen leaned over by me and whispered, "I have something to tell you."

I smiled at her and whispered back, "Should I sit down for this secret?"

With a serious look on her face, she replied, "You might want to, but shut the door first."

So I shut the do to her bedroom and pulled up a chair like she asked. Ellen looked at me with a serious look that

I was not used to seeing. I had no idea where this was headed, so I said a quick prayer. "Lord, please be ready to speak through me if I don't know what to say to her."

Finally, Ellen spoke. "I have been seeing people in my room. I have even been talking to them. Am I going crazy, Jan?"

I sighed a great big sigh of relief, stood up, and kissed her on the forehead, and told her that was perfectly normal. I went on to explain that the closer she got to the end of her journey, since she was looking toward the Lord, He would thin the veil so she could see straight into heaven. Ellen's face lit up like a child at Christmas. Then I went on to explain that loved ones who have passed on before her who are in heaven could come back to visit with her here at the end of her journey. She was so excited she could hardly contain herself. We both had to laugh.

Soon my visit was over. I hugged Ellen and told her to enjoy her company now. She asked if I would please tell her daughter Anna because Ellen was sure she would never believe her. We both smiled and agreed, and I told her I would explain it to her. I kissed her on the forehead and left the room. On my way out, I stopped and explained to Anna about the end of her mother's journey and what she was experiencing. I told Anna that her mother was getting close and I was hoping if Sarah wanted to see her mom before she passed away that she should come for a visit soon. Anna agreed and would see what she could do. We said our good-byes, and I reminded Anna to call if she or Ellen needed anything. Otherwise we would be back in a few days.

When I arrived for my next scheduled appointment, Anna answered the door and announced that Sarah was finally here to see their mom. Anna went on to say Sarah had just flown in this morning and had driven down from the airport just a little while ago, and they could hardly wait to tell Ellen that she was here, but she didn't seem to care. Ellen was too busy looking toward the right corner of the room and excitedly talking to someone they could not see, and not paying any attention to anyone in the room.

Anna said, "It is like we aren't even here."

Following Anna into Ellen's room, I greeted Jeff and got to meet Sarah for the first time. Ellen, of course, was still talking to someone and having a good time. I just went on ahead doing my assessment and getting Ellen's vital signs so I could get finished and out of the family's way, so that they could spend what little time she had left with their mom.

When I had almost finished, Ellen said, "Well hello, Jan. I didn't know you were here. By the way, how am I doing today?"

I replied, "Hello, my sweet friend. You tell me, how are you feeling today?"

Ellen replied quietly, "I feel different. Something has changed about me, but I can't explain it to you. What did you find, Jan?"

I answered, "Ellen, I have never kept anything from you, and I am not going to start now. I see a marked decline today from yesterday, and I don't think you have very long left now."

Ellen responded with a half a grin, "I thought you were going to say that, but please don't tell my husband when he gets back. He worries so much about me. He was just here you know. We talked a long time. He wanted to take me home, but I said it wasn't time for me to come home yet, so he said he would come back in a little while."

I assured Ellen I would not tell him she was sick. I kissed her on the cheek and reminded her how much I loved her as I finished the last of my assessment. The entire visit she did not even seem to notice her family was in the room. She was truly disengaging today.

Before I got the last of my assessment charted, Ellen was excitedly talking to someone new. Her eyes were wide open as she stared up at the right-hand corner of the room. It was all she could do to stay in bed, even as weak as she was. As I smiled and glanced around the room at Ellen's three children, I waited to see their reaction to their mom's enthusiasm. I saw Jeff standing at the head of his mom's bed. Sarah stood beside me, and Anna was at the foot of the bed with a look of shock and disbelief on their faces. I was a little confused at the look but thought maybe they just didn't believe she was seeing loved ones who had passed on before her, even after I had explained to them that when she got this close to death this might happen. So, after several minutes of listening to one-sided conversation from Ellen, Sarah leaned over and asked me if I would please ask who she was talking to. So I did.

I very gently touched Ellen's arm and asked, "Ellen, who are you talking to?"

Ellen finally turned away from the conversation and said with excitement, "You are never going to believe who I am talking to. I am talking to Kara."

No more had the name come out of Ellen's mouth than Sarah fainted onto the floor, right beside me. Ellen did not even notice Sarah had disappeared from the bedside. She had already resumed her conversation with Kara. So, Jeff, Anna, and I assisted Sarah up onto her feet and got her to the other room, where she could sit down comfortably.

Soon Sarah was feeling a little better and Anna began to explain to me what had happened. By what Ellen was saying during her half of the conversation, the kids surmised that it must be Kara that Ellen was talking to. However, Kara was Sarah's twin sister who was tragically killed in a car accident in high school. The family never really healed from that tragedy because they were not allowed to talk about it much. So the memories were very painful, especially for her twin, Sarah. They all agreed it was good to hear it was her, but it was still such a shock. I suggested that the three of them spend as much time in there with their mom as they could, and I suspected she might be talking to a lot of people. She was very wide awake, and they might recognize who she was talking to by her half of the conversation. I also explained to them that during my assessment today it appeared Ellen was in the process of disengaging. What that means is that she was pulling away from what she loved here and was getting ready to leave it behind. Not everyone who is dying does it, but most of them do to some extent, and I am not even sure they know they are doing it. We notice it more on the ones who are wide awake like Ellen versus the ones sleeping all the time. I believe disengaging is just one of those little processes God built into the details of the dying process to help ease the way. Death is as detailed as a birth. That is for sure. God has every detail worked out from start to finish. They seemed more relaxed knowing that was what was going on. I instructed them to call me if they needed me. I was on call otherwise and I would be over in the morning for my scheduled visit.

The next morning when I arrived, Ellen was somnolent, which was completely the opposite of what she was yesterday when I assessed her. Ellen's three children reported that Ellen had been awake and talking to her heavenly visitor most of the night, and they were amazed that they could figure out who they were most of the time by Ellen's half of the conversation. They did add that in between her visitors, they had a chance to talk with her awhile, which seemed to make them all smile. I noticed the children seemed to have an unusual calm about them this morning, which I was very glad to see, because I needed them to accept the fact that Ellen was going to indeed die very soon. I was going to need them to be able to tell their mom that they were going to be all right without her, and that it was okay for her to go. This is very important for the dying to hear from the loved ones. It is like they need permission to go and reassurance that everyone is going to be okay. This is a very difficult point for the family to get to. I excused myself from the living room and went to assess Ellen.

While I was completing the assessment, I noticed Ellen's lower extremities were dusky blue and cold up above her knees. Her blood pressure was very low and her pulse barley palpable. Ellen's body was cool to the touch everywhere and without a doubt starting to shut down. Just as I was finishing the assessment, Ellen woke up and gave me one of her beautiful smiles. As tears filled my eyes, I thought to myself that I was sure going to miss her and that smile.

With a weak voice, she asked, "How am I doing, Jan?"

I smiled and replied, "You feel a little cold to me this

morning. Are you cold, Ellen? Can I get you another blanker?"

Ellen responded, "No thank you. I am toasty warm this morning."

When she answered, I just smiled and looked up and to myself thanked God for another blessing in his intricately detailed death process. Even though her body was getting cold all over, she was feeling warm. So I continued.

"I must tell you that I think you are nearing the end of your journey. Ellen, I believe you might get to go home today."

Ellen smiled and said, "I am so ready to go home. Are you going to be here with me, Jan?"

As I stood leaning over the bedrail holding her cool, dusky, frail hand, I said, "I sure will be if you want me to be, but you have three beautiful children here who would love to be right here with you. I don't think you even need me here."

With a frown, Ellen replied, "Yes, you must be here. I can't do this without you."

I leaned over, kissed her on the forehead, and said, "I think your three children should walk with you to the edge of heaven, and when the Lord feels it is time, He will come and take you by the right hand and take you to heaven with Him to your new home. How does that sound? If you change your mind and think you need me to come back, I am as close as my phone. I am on call."

Ellen smiled and said, "I am going to miss you." I helped her sit up just enough so I could give her what would be our last hug, as I told her how much I loved her and thanked her for sharing her journey with me.

Soon after that, Ellen was all tucked in and sleeping peacefully. I explained to Anna, Sarah, and Jeff that Ellen did not have very long left and that they needed to tell her they were going to be fine here after she was gone and when the Lord came to get her she should go. They were all very tearful, wondering if they would be able to do that and tell her good-bye. I assured them that from what I saw, they loved their mom with all their hearts and would not wish her to have to stay here any longer and suffer, so I was sure they could do it. As I was hugging them good-bye, they tried their best to get me to stay with them. I explained again that I was on call, I lived right here in town, and I was as close as my phone so all they had to do was call me and I would be right back by their side helping them through whatever they needed. Right before I headed for the door, I gathered the three of them together one last time, gave each one a squeeze, and told them, "Take in every single moment of today, because not every child gets the chance to walk their mother to the edge of heaven and hand her off to the Lord. Only the very blessed ones do in my book, and you three are going to be very blessed today. Oh, and by the way, keep alert because when you feel the brush of an angel's wing, you know the Lord is in the room."

8

For Every Life You Have Ever Touched

Each hospice patient that God handpicked to cross my path was as unique as the journey he or she was about to embark on, and this time he handpicked Rosa. Rosa was born and raised in South America, so her accent was incredible, which made listening to her stories so much fun. She had interesting memories to share of when she was young and living with her parents in South America and then exciting stories of when she moved to the United States as a young lady. But her most favorite memories to tell were those of her daughter and grandson, who she spent a great deal of time with. By listening to all of Rosa's stories, one could tell that she was a beautiful person both inside and out. She truly always thought of everyone else first. The longer I knew Rosa, the more I realize that she was one very special lady and must have touched many lives during her lifetime. However, I had no idea just exactly what that meant, and what my sweet Rosa was about to teach me on her final journey.

Rosa had been courageously battling cancer for over two years now, but her fight was nearly over. Rosa was losing the fight. The cancer had taken over Rosa's body despite all the efforts made to stop it. Rosa's oncologist, whom she had become very close to in the last two years, had set up any appointment for Rosa and her daughter, Jackie, to come and reevaluate Rosa's treatment plan.

When they arrived for her appointment, the doctor sat down in front of Rosa, took her now-frail hands in his, and began by saying, "My friend, I believe our fight may be over. We have fought long and hard together, but the cancer is growing so rapidly now the chemo is no longer being effective. I'm hoping if we stop the treatments right now and start treating your symptoms, we could buy you a little quality time to spend with your family without being so sick. You are going to be needing around-the-clock care soon, and I also want you to consider hospice. How does that all sound to you?"

Rosa's frail hands squeezed his big hands as she smiled at him and said, "You are the best. I couldn't have gone through the last two years without you. If this is what you think I need to do, this is what I will do. I feel I could not have survived many more treatments anyway.

I'm so tired. Thank you for all you have done for me. I have a lot to go home and think about."

Rosa let go of the doctor's hands, stood up, and gave him a big, long hug and kissed him lightly on the cheek as if to say good-bye, and she knew it would be the last time she would ever see him. The doctor reminded them that if there was anything she needed, to call him.

After that appointment, Rosa moved in with Jackie, and they immediately got Rosa admitted to hospice. It wasn't long before Rosa's symptoms became manageable. Her nausea and vomiting had stopped almost completely, and her appetite was already showing signs of improvement. It was going to take a little longer than that for Rosa's strength to build up, what little she had left. She was determined to make the most of what life she had left, right up to the very end. Soon that is exactly what Rosa and Jackie did. They began to make the most of every moment. Mother and daughter went on a couple of short trips that had been put on hold earlier because of the cancer treatments. They also spent some memorable time with Rosa's only grandson, David, and his family every chance they got. Rosa had spent a lot of time with her grandson while he was growing up because she watched him during the day while Jackie worked, so Rosa and David had a very special bond. Best of all, Rosa and Jackie spent a lot of time every day meandering down memory lane. They made every minute of Rosa's good days count. However, there were a few days in there when they had to stay home because Rosa was just too weak. It was all she could do to get out of bed and move to the recliner. But in a few days, she was ready to go again. Each time this happened, Jackie could see her mother get a little weaker.

Meanwhile Jackie continued to go to work as was needed, while Rosa was still showing some independence and could manage fine on her own. Jackie's boss was aware that she would eventually need to take a medical leave, but as for right now, she just took days off as she needed them. Rosa and Jackie had enjoyed a good couple of months together, making new memories and remembering old ones. Jackie would treasure this time forever. Jackie could see her mom starting to change. Rosa was growing a little weaker every day, and Jackie had come to the realization that she would never take her mom out again. Rosa was beginning to sleep more during the day, and her appetite was starting to dwindle. There were days when Jackie was lucky to get her to even drink. It was amazing Rosa was still fighting to be independent.

Soon after that, Jackie came home for lunch one day to find Rosa still in bed asleep. Jackie attempted to get Rosa up, but she was too weak. Jackie called hospice, and soon someone was there to help. Together they could get Rosa's cares completed, but Rosa was too weak to sit up. The hospice nurse comforted Jackie, talked with her about a hospital bed, and explained that Rosa had a marked decline overnight and was so weak she might not get out of bed again. They also informed Jackie it was time to quit work. Jackie agreed. As hospice went in the other room to order the hospital bed, Jackie sat in the chair at her mom's bedside and finally broke down and cried. Jackie knew this time was coming, but she just wasn't prepared for it.

From then on Rosa was bedbound, sleeping most of the time and getting steadily weaker. She still had an occasional good day where she would be awake and reminiscing with her daughter about old memories, but those days were slipping away. Hospice increased their visits to three times a week to keep a close eye on her steady decline. On one of our routine hospice visits, Jackie voiced a concern to us about a repeat dream Rosa kept having about a child wrapped in white bandages sitting in a wheelchair at the end of the bed. Rosa would wake up screaming, "Get him away from me." And Jackie would have to go in there and comfort her mother and assure her that she had moved the person in the wheelchair away before Rosa would calm down. This kept happening for about a month, but if Jackie would assure her she had moved him away, Rosa would calm down.

Eventually on one of my routine visits, as I was talking to Rosa and getting her vital signs, she got a frightened look on her face and began to scream, "He is back. Get him away from me, please."

I looked around, and saw no one. I moved to the end of the bed and said, "Rosa, it's all right. I moved him away."

Rosa slowly took her face out of her pillow where she had buried it and stopped yelling. I finished my assessment, and Rosa fell sound asleep. Jackie asked if we could go into the other room and talk a minute.

I said, "Absolutely, what can I do for you?"

Jackie, looking upset said, "Why is my mom being tortured by this vision she keeps seeing at the end of her bed, and today she even saw it when she was wide awake?"

I said, "I am not sure. Do you have a minister you can call, or do you want me to call the hospice chaplain? He is great."

Jackie said, "No, there is enough commotion going on around here."

So I began carefully, "Well, Jackie, it says in the Bible, 'Whenever anyone turns to the Lord, the veil is taken away.' But that is usually when they are very close to death, and they can not only see straight into heaven, they can see and talk to loved ones who have gone before them. Your mom is not that close to death yet, and this is not someone she wants to see, so I am confused. I am sorry I can't help you."

Jackie seemed to be pondering that as we finished

our chat and hugged good-bye. I know I was praying and asking God for some answers and some clarity on this one.

After that Rosa never mentioned the person in the wheelchair at the end of her bed again, and neither did we. It was as if they had vanished or else she was at peace with them being there. I so wanted to ask her about it, but I didn't bring it up for fear of scaring her again. I thought that was going to be a mystery I would never figure out, or would I? I had prayed for God to help me understand, so I could help the patients and their families understand, but this one was going to remain a mystery I guess we were nearing the end of Rosa's journey.

Before too long our hospice visits became daily, Rosa was declining rapidly. One afternoon after my routine visit and assessment, I sat down next to Jackie and explained that Rosa was getting very close, and after my assessment, I felt she only had hours to days left with us now.

Very tearful, Jackie nodded and said, "I knew it was getting close. I don't want her to go, but she has already suffered so much over the last two years."

I gave Jackie a hug, and as she cried on my shoulder, I reminded her that Rosa would be all healed when the Lord came to take her to heaven. Jackie stopped crying and slowly leaned back, and half a smiled crept onto her face, as if that just reminded her that this was not the end for her mom but just the beginning. Rosa was going home. As I walked myself to the door, I turned and remined Jackie I was on call that night, and if she needed anything to give me a call and I would be right over. Jackie gave me a wave to let me know she heard me, but she was still sitting in the same place with the same look on her face.

Later, around midnight my phone rang, and it was Jackie asking me to come over and help her with Rosa. When I arrived, Jackie, looking very exhausted, said, "You must medicate Mom. She is talking crazy and she won't stop. She has been talking all evening and is still talking."

I told Jackie to go take a little break, and I would sit with her mom for a little while. I went over to Rosa's bed, leaned on the rails, and stroked her hair while I listened to what she was saying. When Jackie got out of the shower and was all revived, she came over and asked if I had medicated her.

I said, "No, Jackie, I did not medicate her, and I don't plan on it. I want you to come here and listen to your mom. Your mom is very close now, Jackie, and she is talking to people. We can only hear her half of the conversation, but you can tell it is a conversation if you just listen. I don't know who she is talking to, but you will. You are her daughter. These are your relatives too. So, I want you to sit down in this chair I brought over here for you and listen to your mom's conversations with her loved ones that have passed on before her. They have come back to welcome her home."

Jackie, not saying a word, sat down in the chair I had set up for her and was so intent on listening to her mom that she barley gave me a wave good-bye. I kissed her on the cheek and told her to have fun listening in on the conversations and to call me if she needed me, I was still on call. All she did was nod. I kissed Rosa on the head, whispered, "I love you," told her to have a safe journey if she left before I got back, and I was off, home to get some sleep.

Then at 6:00 a.m., my phone woke me, and it was Jackie yelling on the other end of the phone telling me to come quickly. Now I was anticipating that Jackie had fallen asleep and woke to find her mother had passed away, but it was quite the opposite. When I arrived, Jackie met me in the door shouting excitedly who all her mother had been talking to all night. Rosa had talked to Jackie's father for quite a while, which made Jackie tear up just telling me. Then Jackie named several other relatives she recognized from her mother's half of the conversation. She was so grateful that I did not medicate Rosa and she got to hear all the conversations. Then just like that, Jackie's mood changed.

She looked at me and said, "Do you want to know who that was in the wheelchair at the end of my mom's bed?"

Jackie seemed a little angry and I could not understand

why, but I so wanted to know, so with a little hesitation, I said, "Yes I do."

So Jackie began, "When my son was young, my mom watched him for me while I worked. He came down with the flu and was dehydrated, so they had to put him in the hospital for a few days on IV fluids. My mom stayed there with him while I worked. Well, across the hall was a little boy who was hurt very bad in a car accident, and he was wrapped head to toe in bandages, and every day while my son was napping, my mom would walk across the hall and read to him. When my son was well enough to leave the hospital, and go back to school, my mom continued to go to the hospital every day and read to the little boy. One day when she went to the hospital to read to him, he was not there, and when she asked where he was, they told her he had died. The little boy's name was Zachary, and I was listening to my mom's conversations last night. She talked to him several different times. My mom was so happy to hear from him. I thought you told me that everyone that went to heaven was healed. Zachary wasn't. My mom saw him in his bandages and wheelchair at the end of her bed."

By this time, Jackie was in tears and was yelling at me, waiting for me to answer, and it's for this very reason I pray before I ever enter a patient's home. I pray for God to speak through me to my patients and their families that have tough questions they need answers to in their time of grief that I cannot answer. This was no different.

I said a quick prayer, and I began by saying, "Jackie, everyone is healed when they get to heaven. However, when your mom saw him in the wheelchair at the end of the bed, that was several weeks ago, and she was not close enough to the end of her journey to see into heaven yet. When he visited her while she was still here, on this side of heaven, she had to see him exactly how she saw him the last time so she could recognize who she was seeing. However, when she saw him last night when she talked to him, she was seeing right into heaven, and she was seeing him without his bandages and all healed, and she knew immediately who he was. Another one of God's promises."

At first Jackie just sat there thinking about what I said, and then slowly a smile brightened her face as she said, "They are healed in heaven, aren't they?"

I nodded my head and replied, "Yes, Jackie, God has promised that all who go to heaven will be healed."

By now Jackie's smile was brightening the room, and the anger was gone. With excitement in her voice, Jackie began once again sharing stories of her mom's amazing conversations during the night. Jackie shared with me that her father had been a professional musician back in his day, and in one of the conversations he must have told Rosa he was playing last night and wished she was there with him.

With tears welling up in her eyes, Jackie said, "My mom told him she was sorry she couldn't be there last night, but that she would be home tomorrow."

I got up and gave Jackie a big hug as she cried on my shoulder. She had been up so many hours with her mom and she was exhausted, but there was no way she was going to leave her side now, so I suggested Jackie to go take a couple-hour break while I gave Rosa a nice bath, changed her bedding, and repositioned her so she was already for Jackie to just sit beside the bed and hold her hand. Jackie smiled and headed for her room.

While I was bathing Rosa, she would wake for a few minutes and talk to me, and then would be back to sleep. I had a chance to tell her how much she meant to me and how much I was going to miss her. I told her that I understood she had a lot of visitors last night, and she just smiled. I asked her how Zachary was.

She opened her eyes and said, "He is just fine now."

And off to sleep she went. I just smiled to myself. As I continued to lotion my little Rosa up and enjoy the quiet time I had with her, it hit me—it is not just your loved ones who have passed on before you that come in and out to see you when your close to death, or that wait in a crowd ready to cheer when the Lord brings you home. It is also the lives you have touched while you were down here living your life. So for every life a person has ever touched, they too will be there to greet you I said in a whisper, "Thank you, Lord. Now I know why you picked this angel to cross my path. She had something to teach me. I love you."

Eventually I finished the bath, changing the bed and the repositioning. When I had her exactly where I wanted her, all surrounded in a cloud of pillows and comfortable, I leaned over and kissed Rosa on the forehead, and when she opened her eyes, I told her, "I want to thank you for all you have taught me, and to tell you how much I love you. I don't want you to be scared about a thing. The Lord is going to come and take you by the hand and take you home where there is no more cancer, pain, sorrow, or tears. He has promised us that, but you know that, and best of all, there will be a crowd of people waiting to welcome you home, including your loved ones who have gone on before you. My dear, for every life you have touched, they will be there to greet you home too. Rosa, I am guessing you have touched a lot of lives my sweet angel, so be ready when the Lord takes you home. Your homecoming will be epic."

Rosa smiled and said, "I love you, and I will see you again."

I kissed her forehead one more time as I pulled the covers up around her, knowing I would never see her again on this side. My heart was heavy as always, but I could not wish a one of them back as sick as they were, if there was no cure. I would be selfish not to be happy about them going home to be with the Lord.

Soon Jackie was refreshed and ready to sit with her mom again. Before I left, I explained to her what I had learned. Jackie smiled and agreed Rosa had touched a lot of lives in her life as she tried to imagine her mom's homecoming when the Lord came to take her home. Jackie's eyes were teary, but the smile was radiant. She knew her mom was ready to go home, and it was time to let go. I hugged Jackie one last time and reminded her to call me when her mom's condition changed or if she needed anything. Jackie agreed, and I left to start my day.

After a few hours, I was called back to Jackie's. When I arrived, I could see Rosa had already passed away.

Jackie said, "I was holding her hand. She was talking to different people off and on. Then she became very quiet, and her breathing slowed and stopped."

I gave Jackie a hug and told her that we pray for peaceful deaths like this. Jackie said, "But I didn't have time to call you. I didn't want to be here by myself."

I smiled and said, "Well, your mom wanted you to walk her to the edge of heaven by yourself, without me, and she knew you could do it, and she was right. Furthermore, Rosa and I had already said our good-byes earlier when I was giving her a bath. She said she would see me again someday; she knew it wouldn't be today."

Jackie was smiling through her tears as we hugged, and I knew she was going to be just fine.

What I really want to know is, how was the homecoming, Rosa?

Whenever anyone turns to the Lord, the veil is taken away. (2 Corinthians 3:16 NIV)

For it will not be you speaking, but the Spirit of your Father speaking through you. (Matthew 10:20 NIV)

9

Through the Eyes of a Child

I was on my way to the last patient visit of the day. Today had been a very long and trying day. If something could go wrong, it did, and I'm not even sure why. My other three patients were doing very well today. I was one of those positive people who always saw the glass as half full. I always had a smile to give away, and I could cheer up anyone. But not today. Everything seemed to get on my last good nerve. I was a master at never letting my patient or their family see an irritable side of me. I always prayed God would help me leave any problem I was dealing with outside and make the visit all about the patient, and He has never let me down. Even if I was successful in keeping it from the patient and his or her family, I knew I was in a bad mood, and I hated it. What was wrong with me today? Why was today so hard?

Where was God today? Had He even shown up for work today?

I finally arrived at my patient Katherine's house. If anything was going to make me smile today, this should. Katherine had been living with her daughter, Lizzy, since she had gotten sick, and Lizzy's yard was a little piece of heaven on earth. Lizzy told me, before Katherine got sick, that Lizzy and her mom used to spend hours out there working in the yard planting flowers. There were stargazer lilies, hollyhocks, asters, snapdragons, and garden phlox as far as the eye could see, and that was just the front yard. Then around back, there was a big pond with a walking path around it. Along the path were a lot more flower gardens and benches scattered here and there so you could sit and take in all the serenity it had to offer. I just stood out there a minute or two and inhaled the smell of the flowers to try to sweeten this bad mood before anyone got a glimpse of it. This was truly the sweetest family, along with Katherine, Lizzy's daughter, Karla, and her daughter, Brittney, were living with Lizzy while Karla's husband was overseas. I always felt this house was blessed. It had four generations of women living under one roof.

Katherine was only in her seventies but was at the very end stages of her disease process when we received the order to admit her to hospice. Unfortunately for us, Katherine was already sleeping twenty out of twenty-four hours a day. We rarely got to talk with her. In fact, most visits we were lucky to get a hello out of her, and today was no different. We got to know Katherine only through her daughter, and the stories she shared with us. We learned that Katherine was a good Christian and always went to church. It appeared to us that Lizzy was a good Christian too, by the Bible on the end table and the cross hanging on the wall, but she had never talked about it. I was praying for God to start that conversation so I did not overstep my boundaries with Lizzy.

Katherine was sleeping when I started my assessment of her. Even when I rolled her to check her skin on her back and bottom and repositioned her onto her other side, she never woke up. I finished my physical assessment and then asked if I could talk with Lizzy and Karla for a minute. We sat down, and I explained to them some of the signs I was seeing when I was completing my assessment. I told them I had noted a definite decline in her condition, and I thought we were looking at hours to maybe days left now before she passed. This news seemed to come as such a shock to Lizzy, even though she knew that her mom did not have long to live when we signed her onto hospice. I guess it is just the shock of hearing those words when it is about your mother. I asked Lizzy or Karla if they had any questions, and they had several. I answered their questions to the best of my ability, and when we had finished, gave them all the support I knew how. This family needed so much support. Just ten short months ago, Lizzy's brother Jimmy died of lung cancer, and that blow came just about the time Katherine got her diagnosis. This family was no amateur when it came to loss, and it was about to happen again. I had been praying faithfully for this family to find some peace in all of this, but it had not come. I prayed, "God, this family needs a miracle. They need to know you are here among us and going to be taking her home when it's your perfect time, where she has the promise of healing and eternal life with you, Lord.' I was not sure where their faith stood right now, and I was afraid to ask. I prayed for God to open the door to that conversation for me and make it soon.

The mood of the room changed completely when the bedroom door flung open, and in came Brittney. The bouncing blond three-year-old belonged to Karla.

"Hi," Brittney said, "what's your name?"

I reminded her that my name was Jan and that she met me the last time I was here to see her great-grandma. "Oh," she said as she came bounding over, jumped in my lap, and began to tell me all about her day. I thought to myself, *Oh to be a three-year-old again, not a care in the world. How amazing.* I looked over at Lizzy and Karla to see their first smiles of the visit. As Brittney sat chattering on my lap, I said a quick prayer to God to thank him for the smiles he provided to the room through this beautiful little three-year-old. Brittney jumped down out of my lap and began to play on the floor with some of her toys.

So, as I began to gather up my stuff and get ready to leave, I reminded Lizzy that I was the nurse on call that night, and if she needed anything to be sure to call me. Lizzy hugged me good-bye, with a hug that seemed to last forever. My heart ached. I wanted so bad to take away some of her pain. That I could not do, but my God could, and I was praying.

As Lizzy walked me slowly to the door, we heard Brittney let out an excited squeal. "Well hello, Uncle Jimmy," the little voice shrieked. "Where have you been?"

Lizzy and I froze in our tracks. I motioned for Lizzy to be quiet as we slowly turned around and saw Karla hurrying into the room from the kitchen. I motioned to Karla to *shhhhhh*, and with a nod, I knew she understood. Brittney had run up to the empty wooden rocking chair that sat beside Katherine's bed. This rocking chair was put there for company to sit in when they came to visit with Katherine. We all stood frozen in time as Brittney carried on this very excited, one-sided conversation with her deceased great-uncle Jimmy. She must have talked about something that made sense to Lizzy and Karla because the tears rolled down their cheeks at the same time. I just kept motioning for them to be quiet.

After what seemed to be several minutes, Brittney

said, "Good-bye, Uncle Jimmy. I will see you later," and she went back to playing as if nothing had happened. Lizzy and Karla looked at me as if they had seen a ghost. I quietly told Lizzy to ask Brittney who she was talking too. She did, and Brittney responded, "I was talking to Uncle Jimmy. He is here to see Great-Grandma. He is waiting for her."

Brittney jumped up and ran in her room to play with her dolls, and that was my chance to have a talk with Lizzy and Karla. While they were getting Brittney settled, I had a chance to pray and thank God for sending a three-year-old with the miracle that I needed to open the door to tell these two about the journey Katherine was on to heaven. I also had to apologize. God did show up for work today. I had just forgotten to talk to Him.

When Lizzy and Karla came back, we talked about what had happened. I explained that Katherine was getting so close to dying that what I like to call little miracles were happening. People who have passed on before you come back as angels to see you and ready you for your trip. The Bible says that when you are close to death, if you look toward the Lord, the veil will be thinned so you can look into heaven. So I explained that if Katherine was awake and talking, she would be telling us all the beautiful sights and colors she was seeing right now. She would be telling us all the people she was getting to talk to. I told them, to me, if you are a Christian, death is spectacular. They both looked at me with hesitation.

I explained, "Yes, if Katherine could be healed here on earth, that is what we would want, but there is not a cure, so you can't wish her to stay here with all this pain and discomfort, can you? Don't you want her to go home to be with the Lord for all eternity where she is healed?"

Lizzy and Karla were crying but agreed that they could not wish her to stay in this terminal state.

Out of nowhere, Lizzy asked, "How did Brittney see Jimmy?"

With a smile, I responded it was because she was an innocent child. If only us adults could trust like a child and see life through their eyes. The Bible says in Matthew 19:14, "But Jesus said, 'Let the little children come to me and do not hinder them, for to such belongs the kingdom of heaven.'"

I stayed until Lizzy and Karla seemed to be accepting of the fact that Katherine was going home to be with her Lord very soon. They had asked lots of questions, and with God's help as always, I could give them an answer. God always spoke for this hospice nurse if a family asked a tough question about death and after life that I had no answer for. I pray every day before I go into each patient's home for Him to speak through me when I need Him. He had never let me down, and today was no different. I realized on this visit, God was at work today. I just never bothered to look for Him at the other three patients I visited. No wonder I was having a bad day.

Lizzy called me in the night to say she could not get her mom comfortable. I explained I would be there in thirty minutes. When I arrived, I noted Katherine was mottled from her toes to her knees, and they were cold. Her respirations were weak, her pulse low, and her blood pressure almost nonexistent. Katherine was so close. I believe Lizzy knew her mom was close and did not want to be there alone. So I gave her a bed bath, changed her linens, and began to reposition her with pillows so she appeared to be as comfortable as if she was floating on a cloud. She did not look to be in any pain, and there was no anxiety. She looked as peaceful as she possibly could. I thought I would just wait a little while and see if Lizzy calmed down. Just then the bedroom door opened, and out came Karla and Brittney. I guess we had woken them up. Karla looked very nervous to see me in the middle of the night, but Lizzy quickly explained that she had called me just to come and help get Katherine comfortable.

An hour passed, and Katherine was still holding her own. Lizzy decided it was silly to make me stay any longer. She was going to be fine. She said I should go home and get some sleep before work tomorrow and that Karla and Brittney should go back to bed. Everybody agreed that was a good idea.

As I gathered my things, I was telling Lizzy what to

watch for when out of nowhere Brittney shrieked, "Look at all of Great-Grandma's friends that came to see her." She was waving her hand over her head in the direction of Katherine's bed. Brittney was so excited that she was jumping up and down and clapping wildly. We all looked around the room at each other and smiled. The tears were running down everyone's cheeks like rain. I quickly went over to Katherine's bed just in time to see her open her eyes. I called Lizzy and Karla to the bed and told them to tell her good-bye. The Lord was on His way. I was just about sure of that. He was going to take her right hand now, and she was going home to heaven. They rushed over, each taking one of Katherine's hands. They told her how much they loved her and that they were going to be fine, and that Brittney told them that all her friends were here to see her off. Katherine gave a little smile, breathed her last breath, and was gone. Wow, you could just feel the energy in the room. There must have been angels everywhere. Remember, when you feel the brush of an angel's wing, you know that the Lord is in the room. Once again, I was standing on hallowed ground in the Lord's presence. Right at that very moment I realized this was more than a job; it was a calling.

When Lizzy and Karla were ready to leave Katherine's bed, I gave them both a big hug and said, "Do you two know what you just did?" They shook their heads no. I said, "You just walked Katherine to the edge of heaven and handed her off to the Lord. You two were just standing on hallowed ground. The Lord was right here in this room."

Lizzy and Karla smiled as they hugged each other tight. In a few minutes, after it soaked in, Lizzy looked at Karla and with a tear on her cheek said, "Mom is in heaven with Jimmy now."

This is exactly what this family needed to begin to heal. God used a child to show Lizzy and Karla that Jimmy and Katherine were safe in his arms now in heaven. God gave this family the peace and closure they needed to heal. He always delivers what we need. I am guessing Lizzy and Karla will never view death the same after this experience.

In the meantime, Brittney, the little bouncy blond, was already back to playing with her toys. The excitement was all over for this three-year-old. She had already done what God had planned for her to do—just be innocent like children naturally are. If we could all only see life through the eyes of a child.

> When Jesus saw this, He was indignant. He said to them, "Let the little children come to Me, and do not hinder them, for the kingdom of God belongs to such as these. Truly I tell you, anyone who will not receive the kingdom of God like a little child will

never enter it. And He took the children in His arms, placed His hands on them and blessed them. (Mark 10:14–16 NIV)

A NOTE FROM THE AUTHOR

Thank you for taking the time to read my book. These were just a few of the many wonderful memories I have that the Lord picked for me to write about in this book. I hope the information blesses and teaches you as much as it has blessed and taught me. As I said in my book, I feel hospice was not just a job for me, it was a calling, and I believe it took writing this book for me realize that. God not only answered my questions I had about death and heaven, but he also taught me more things about being a Christian than I ever dreamed of.

You are all probably wondering why I am not doing hospice anymore when I love it so much. Well, as I said in my book, it is a calling, and I believe if I am supposed to be called back working with the dying in one way or another, the Lord will open that door for me again. As for right now, he has me on another path. You see, five years ago I wrote God a letter, folded it up, and put it in my Bible. Well, he answered it!

So I had a few tough decisions to make. Then I took one big leap of faith, and no He did not let me fall; the Lord taught me how to fly.

You will never guess where I am now!

Remember to trust in the Lord with all your heart and nothing is impossible.

Blessings to all,

Love,

Jan

Trust in the Lord with all your heart, and do not lean on your own understanding. (Proverbs 3:5)

ABOUT THE AUTHOR

Jan was frightened of death and confused about heaven at a very young age. No matter who she asked, the answer was never acceptable. Being a Christian she felt an empty fear in her heart when she thought about death, she needed answers. So, she prayed. When she became a nurse, death was a normal part of the job at times, and this became very difficult. She prayed for God to please take her fear of death, and her confusion of heaven away so she could be more help to her patients, whom she dearly loved. After a couple of years and obviously the work of the Lord, Jan was put into a position where she needed to take the hospice job. She assured them that she would not be there long because she had a fear of death. The boss assured Jan they had chosen the right person for the job. What Jan didn't know was this was the answer to her prayers she had been praying for years. What God was about to show her was going to change her life forever. She stayed there for eleven years. She is no longer scared of death or dying, and is not confused about heaven. Actually, sitting with one of her dying patients is where she finds the most comfort, and right there on hallowed ground is where she feels the closest to the Lord.

Printed in the United States
By Bookmasters